Gros Morne

A LIVING LANDSCAPE

Pat McLeod

BREAKWATER

©1988 Pat McLeod

Canadian Cataloguing in Publication Data

McLeod, Pat
    Gros Morne : a living landscape

Includes index.
ISBN 0-920911-37-4 (bound)– ISBN 0-920911-36-6 (pbk.)

1. Gros Morne National Park (Nfld.) — Description. I. Title.

FC2164.G76M34 1987   917.18   C87-090225-3
F1124.G76M34 1987

Lines from Edith Sitwell, ``Sailor, What of the Isles?'' from *Selected Poems* (Macmillan: 1965) reprinted by kind permission of the author and the publisher.

Unless otherwise credited, photographs on cover and throughout book by Pat McLeod.

Maps by Sam Crowley, Peregrine Corporation.

Breakwater gratefully acknowledges the financial support of The Canada Council which has helped make this publication possible.

The Publisher acknowledges the financial contribution of the Cultural Affairs Division of the Department of Culture, Recreation and Youth, Government of Newfoundland and Labrador which has helped make this publication possible.

How is it possible, in this flat world, to know
Why South should be below, the North above?

Edith Sitwell

Dedication

For the people of Bonne Bay who have taught me, among so
many other things, that 'Down' is North.

Contents

Foreword

Who can say he knows Canada who has not stood on the shore of the Pacific with the great mountains of the Western Cordillera at his back and the limitless ocean beyond? Who can say he knows Canada who has not travelled over the great plains and realized the big country between the distant horizons, and heard the wind rustle the grasses and sing in the wires? Or seen the limitless forests and countless beautiful lakes of the ancient glacially-scoured Shield? Or looked from the gracious valleys to the gentle hills of the eastern seaboard provinces? Who can say he knows this country who has not seen the Atlantic rollers, refugees from storms a thousand miles away, crashing endlessly on the Scotian shore? And beyond, still eastward, who can say he knows this land who has not marvelled at the enormous cliffs and deep lakes along the western fringe of Newfoundland, and seen the whales and seals swirl among the schools of fish in the deep arms of the sea that reach far into the land? Here, we now know of an incredible story of continents drifting, of oceans opening and closing, and fragments of deep ocean bottoms uplifted to make astonishing moonscapes among ancient Shield rocks and limestones of gentler seas.

This book is the work of an unusual traveller in this wonderful piece of eastern Canada, the area set aside as Gros Morne National Park. It is by one who knows the country and its people, and who feels at one with the nature of the place. A writer who spices descriptions of the physical features of the country with stories of its history, with personal encounters with the environment, with deep-felt sympathy with the whole of the natural scene.

Reading it will show you glimpses of a most impressive part of Canada, and, if you have travelled there before, as have I so many times, it will recall these places with warming pleasure.

David M. Baird
Portland, Ontario

7

Preface

This is a book of Gros Morne, in all its moods and in every season, a place of splendid landscapes and waterscapes, all full of living things, and for me it is also a place to live. As well as trying to bring these landscapes to life in words and photographs, I have given some background on the enclave communities of the Park and their people, past and present, for they are as much a part of the place as are its mountains and inlets. I hope this book will be a companionable one to take along on the travels it may entice you to make.

I am not a professional in any of the fields usually associated with the great outdoors, but I relish my small store of layman's knowledge of the world of nature and have tried to share with others the joys of discovery and the sheer sensory impact of this place in which I have lived these many years. If my feelings run away with my pen, or my descriptions occasionally trespass on current thought in, say, geology, I can only say that good friends have helped me try to get things right, and all the errors are mine alone.

Inevitably, in writing about terrain, the matter of distances comes up, and I have had to make a choice between the well-worn Anglo-Saxon words that flow so comfortably from my tongue and pen, and the accurate but foreign words of the metric system. My simple prose makes no literary claims, but when describing the landscape, I have chosen the words that feel as much at home there as I do myself, rather than those that seem to belong to a different world. As precise accuracy was less important than the creation of a feeling and an image in the mind of the reader, the only place you will find metric measurements is on the twin scales of distance to be found on the maps.

The book is based on eighteen years spent as weaver, craft shop operator, occasional freelance writer and photographer, and extensive wilderness traveller. It is mainly a very personal account of what has delighted, awed, or interested me in my life here and in my travels through nearly all of this marvellous area.

In writing this book, I have many people to thank, but for the years and the experiences on which it is based I must first acknowledge the kindred spirit with whom I have shared them, Gisela Westphalen. Different in many ways, the factor that drew us both to take up the challenge of living by our own efforts in rural Newfoundland was a shared wish to step off the beaten track of life with its organizations, hierarchies and repetitive routines. The experiment demanded more of our time and effort than any ordinary job, but proved surprisingly successful and has given each of us some of the best years of our lives. As well as sharing the experiences, Gisela has encouraged me to write this account of them and has helped at every stage by contributing memories, correcting details and pruning my burgeoning adjectives. It is in many ways as much her book as mine.

Clyde Rose of Breakwater Books, my publisher and summertime neighbour, provided the impetus and encouragement to get me started, and I thank him for trusting me to write about this very special place, Gros Morne, which is as dear to him as it is to me.

Al Pittman, with whose poetry I feel so much in tune, has edited the manuscript with more grace and patience than I deserved, and I thank him most warmly for his help.

Without Linda Coates' ability to read my writing, and expertly type both first and final drafts, I doubt my manuscript would ever have reached the publisher. I am much indebted to her.

Friends who read and gave me helpful comments on my first draft were Don and Isobel Learmonth, Beverley and Glen Kirby, and Tony Berger, who also provided advice on the geology. Don Lockwood, Superintendent of Gros Morne National Park, has been generous with his help and support, reading and commenting on the manuscript, giving me free run of the Park's library, and some helicopter time for otherwise unobtainable photographs. Jeff Anderson of the Park staff has helped by supplying me with books and information, and Anna Kearney's book *Getting To Know Ourselves*, written for Parks Canada, has been a useful historical reference. Until her death in 1985, Ella Manuel was a much valued friend and a fount of knowledge about Newfoundland in general and Bonne Bay in particular. Her little book, *Bonne Bay 1800-1900* has been a valuable source of Bonne Bay history. Em Tapper has likewise been both a storehouse of local knowledge and a staunch friend.

I am much indebted to Dr. David Baird for writing the Foreword to this book. As one-time government geologist in Newfoundland, he was the writer of a 1958 letter to then-Premier J.R. Smallwood suggesting that the Bonne Bay area should become a national park. Thus Dr. Baird can well be regarded as the prime mover in the establishment of Gros Morne National Park. I am honoured to have his support.

Lastly, but by no means least important, I would like to thank the many friends in Bonne Bay, and especially our nearest neighbours, the two Taylor families, for making us feel so much at home in Curzon Village and in the old house by the shore.

P.McL

Gouged by ice and water, Newfoundland's Western Brook Pond can well be compared with Norway's west coast scenery.

A Quality of Westerliness

Whether it's the way the world spins, or the effects of the afternoon sun on the glaciers long ago, or the forces that wrench the continents this way and that, there seems to be some factor that creates a repeating pattern of terrain on west coasts.

Mountain ranges run north and south, parallel to the coastline. Deep inlets and fjords run out to the sea, carved by the glaciers and by aeons of erosion. Norway, Southern Chile, New Zealand's South Island, British Columbia, Scotland, all watch the sun set in the western ocean and have this high and magnificent coastal scenery.

Some of those west coasts have mountains that are the spires and roof-peaks of the world. Others have older mountains, rounded by weather and erosion over countless millennia. They are less dramatic, but with the salt water at their feet the eye can encompass their full height at a glance.

So it is in the hills of my childhood, the West Highlands of Scotland. Ben Nevis, whose summit is a mere 4400 feet, stands so close to the shores of its sea-loch that it rivals far greater mountains in its fierce and dramatic character.

And so it is here, where Newfoundland's highest mountains meet the sea at Bonne Bay, halfway up the long west coast. Gros Morne, ancient, grey and rounded like an elephant's back, stands out from the main range and sweeps down to the deep waters of the East Arm. Its looming presence dominates the area, and with the Tableland, Killdevil, and the mountains of Western Brook Pond, creates a quality of westerliness to compare with the far bigger terrain of Norway, Scotland or New Zealand.

Here, in this most special place, so diverse in its scenery, so distinguished in its flora, fauna and geology, and so rich in the humanity of its inhabitants, Canada's Gros Morne National Park was created in 1973. And here, in this same special place, I have lived, and relished living, for the past eighteen years of my life.

Gisela Westphalen

Climbing Gros Morne, the double fjord of Bonne Bay and the Tableland fill the view to the south.

CHAPTER 1

From the Top of Gros Morne: An Overview

Gros Morne, Newfoundland's most famous mountain and, at 2644 feet, the island's second highest, is in the very centre of Gros Morne National Park. The fine trail that leads to its top and around by the side valley is an arduous full day's hike. On the way, the hiker may meet with any kind of weather, encounter almost any of the Park's wildlife, and, once on the top, scan a great deal of the Park's terrain.

Due west spreads the coast, with the town of Rocky Harbour strung around a bay, a lighthouse prominent at its northern tip. The Park headquarters is located close to the town which is the largest of the enclave communities in the Park area.

The highway hugs the coastline running north. Between the shore and the mountains, the coastal plain of bogs and innumerable ponds gradually widens till, at the north end of the Park, the mountains are some ten miles inland.

Immediately below Gros Morne on the north side is a deep cleft containing Ten Mile Pond. Beyond it are a whole series of these clefts carved out by glaciers and erosion over the millennia. The most dramatic of them is Western Brook Pond, where cliffs the full height of the Long Range drop to a great body of water some twelve miles long. The gorge there is one of the highlights of the Park and the boat ride between the cliffs is a breathtaking experience. It was once a true fjord, filled by the sea, and one cannot help comparing it to the great fjords of Norway.

Further up the coast are three more fishing communities, enclaves within the Park: Sally's Cove, on the open shore; St. Paul's, within the estuary of St. Paul's Inlet; and Cow Head, on a bay sheltered by the distinctive Cow Head Peninsula. Just short of the boundary is a long crescent of sandy beach called Shallow Bay. Its white sand, backed by dunes and forest, provides a complete contrast to the rest of the Park's terrain.

Viewed from the top of Gros Morne, a great bay fills the foreground from the west to the southeast. This double fjord is Bonne Bay. It has long been known for its extraordinary beauty, and had much to do with the decision to establish a national park in this area. The six-mile Western Arm is the famous one, with its blend of dramatic mountains and pretty communities strung along the shore. The uninhabited Main, or East Arm, runs from the foot of Gros Morne eight miles to the southeast with the splendidly scenic highway following its eastern shore.

13

Between the two arms of Bonne Bay is high forested country. The Bonne Bay road (Route 431) runs through its handsome scenery and drops steeply down to wind along the Western Arm. On the north shore of the bay, closest to Gros Morne, the widespread community of Norris Point lies over rolling ground, around small coves, and beside a landlocked inlet to form a most attractive town.

Across the water from Norris Point, the community of Woody Point catches the light and stands out against a remarkable skyline. A huge plateau of totally contrasting colour stands clear and separate from all the forested hills round about. This is the Tableland and it is indeed different from its surroundings, for the colossal forces of the moving continents thrust up a great chunk of the earth's mantle from the deep ocean floor and left it overlapping the crust. The red-gold plateau looks completely arid and bare, but although most of the normal groundcover cannot grow here, it has its own unique range of plants, many of them rare and all of them able to survive in a sub-arctic winter climate.

The Tableland, together with the valley, known as The Gulch, at the foot of the steep escarpment, is perhaps the most unusual and interesting terrain in Newfoundland. Running through The Gulch is the road to Trout River, a busy, scenic fishing community, full of character. Just inland from the town lie the two Trout River Ponds bounded on the north side by the Tableland and on the south by the contrasting hills of the Gregory Plateau. The Trout River road also passes the head of the Green Gardens trail, one of the Park's finest hikes, which leads down to an area of lush green meadows between the forest and high volcanic cliffs where the open Gulf of St. Lawrence beats on the shore below.

Away to the southeast, at the foot of the big Main Arm, is a gem of a spot called Lomond, now a Park day area and camp site — a lovely place to visit and spend a day, or two or three. Across the water from Lomond stands Killdevil, a mountain nearly as high as Gros Morne, whose bold stripes of vegetation and coloured rock give it a character all its own.

Inland, beyond Gros Morne lies the rolling plateau of the Long Range. It is caribou and arctic hare country. Nearly every top is a grazing area of caribou moss. Moose are up there, too, but they prefer the wooded valleys between the tops. This high wilderness stretches for forty or fifty miles across the peninsula till the land drops down to White Bay on the other side.

These glimpses reveal some of the special places of the Park, and are an invitation to explore — on foot, by car, or by boat — the marvellous terrain over which Gros Morne presides.

CHAPTER 2

The Southeast Corner

Wiltondale, Point of Decision

Driving down to Gros Morne National Park from Deer Lake, you come upon a small community surrounded by hills and forest, a little lumbering settlement called Wiltondale. The name comes from its pioneer settler, Norman Wilton, one of the family of that name in Woody Point. In 1927 he and his wife and young children moved from that community and settled near the remote junction of foot trails and cart tracks. For a number of years they lived there alone. The household was an hospitable and much valued one where travellers were always sure of a meal and a place to sleep on their way through the country.

Attracted by the chance to make an independent living in the lumberwoods, additional families moved there over the years. The decade of the 1960s brought work to the area and more settlers moved in as the new Northern Peninsula highway was constructed, over the mountains to the north of Wiltondale and along the shore of the East Arm of Bonne Bay.

With the creation of the Park in 1973 the little community of Wiltondale suddenly found itself the gateway to one of Canada's greatest national parks. Located as it is just outside the boundary of the Park, at the junction of the Northern Peninsula highway (Route 430) and the Bonne Bay road (Route 431), it is the point of access for both the northern and the southwestern sections of the Park.

Apart from lumbering, there is not much employment in Wiltondale, but some good amenities have been built under recent employment programs. The first such project, in 1977, was to provide an interdenominational church for the community. To make way for Park facilities, Lomond was being cleared of houses and one of these was a recently built A-frame. As it was too wide to be transported over the narrow bridges of the Lomond road, it was floated across the Main Arm to Rocky Barachois and put aboard a flatbed trailer. The group of carpenters, which included two able women, set it up beside the school in Wiltondale and converted it into a small church. A handsome building, it is well used and has done much to give the town both the look and the feel of an established community.

A more recent enterprise has been the creation of a museum and replica pioneer village. To house the museum, another of the disused homes of Lomond, one dating

15

from the 1920s heyday of that little lumbering town, was taken apart and reassembled in Wiltondale. Around it were built a schoolhouse, church, store and workshed, and all were furnished with an interesting collection of artifacts, furniture, tools and memorabilia, lent or donated by people all around the Bonne Bay area. One of the bedrooms of the museum house has a unique exhibit of special interest to weavers, or anyone interested in textiles: the room is furnished from floor to ceiling with soft furnishings woven by an active weaving group known as Bonne Bay Weavers.

For the traveller, Wiltondale is the place at which to decide which section of the Park to see first. Since all of Gros Morne is worth seeing, and there are plenty of camping areas, it is best to organize your stay so as to have time to explore both the northern and southwestern sections of the Park.

Lomond

Lomond and the Lomond River were named after Loch Lomond in Scotland by the Scottish manager of the St. Lawrence Timber, Pulp and Shipping Company which ran a large lumbering operation there from the 1920s to the late '40s. It was then operated by the Bowater's Newfoundland Pulp and Paper Mills Limited until operations ceased in the 1950s.

The first mill was set up in Stanleyville, but moved to nearby Lomond in 1918 because of the lack of room for expansion at the original site. As well, the Lomond River and its estuary were valuable for driving and storing logs, and the deep water of the Main Arm of Bonne Bay allowed ocean-going vessels to come close to shore.

From Lomond ran the first connection to the railhead at Deer Lake, some thirty miles away. In summer this was a rough cart track; in winter the journey was made by dog team. The many communities around Bonne Bay were connected to Lomond by a ferry service, run by various enterprising individuals over the years. Travellers from the northwest coast would come by boat to Lomond, travel through the country to Deer Lake, and continue east by rail to St. John's or west to Bay of Islands or Port aux Basques.

Lomond was a typical company town with trim little houses for the employees and a fine house, now Killdevil Lodge, for the manager. The mill — the largest in Newfoundland and larger than any in eastern Canada at the time — and its cutting operation employed over four hundred men. The St. Lawrence Company was cutting virgin forest at first, and among the lumber they exported were axe-squared baulks of pine up to three feet square. But as the work continued, available trees became progressively smaller until, in the end, their main export was shiploads of pit-props for the British mines. Later, when Bowaters took over the operation, they sent cord-wood to the paper mill in Corner Brook.

When the mill finally closed the premises and houses were sold and Lomond became a favourite place for summer cabins. The mill manager's house became, for several years, a lodge for salmon anglers and tourists. Later it was purchased by the Anglican Church, which still maintains the house and land as a camp ground for young people. With this function, the name Killdevil Lodge became singularly appropriate!

Over the years, the lush meadows of Lomond became known as an excellent place to graze horses. From all around Bonne Bay and Trout River, people took their horses there to get fat and sleek over the summer. There were dozens of them there when I first visited the place and camped near the site of the old mill. Chatting one evening to an old gentleman who had one of the company houses for a summer cabin, I asked how so many horses came to be at Lomond. He replied, "Maid, dere's t'ousands of 'em. The horiginal 'arse was borned 'ere!"

When the Park took over Lomond, all remaining buildings were removed to make way for the camp grounds and day-use areas we enjoy today. The horses were officially banished, but any loose horse in the district will still travel miles to get to those familiar green meadows!

The approach to Lomond is by a winding gravel road with glimpses of glittering water and the steep flank of Killdevil to be seen through the trees. Where the houses once stood, all is now green meadow backed by tree-covered hills, running down to a pebble beach and crystal-clear water.

The Lomond camp ground is perhaps the most scenic one in the Park. The sites have marvelous views of the East Arm and Killdevil. There is much to do in the immediate area, and it is an excellent base from which to drive, hike and explore the whole southeast and southwest sections of the Park extending from Killdevil mountain to Trout River on the coast.

Near the campsite is a lovely short hiking trail that takes you over a ridge and down into the next cove, to the original site of Stanleyville. It is an idyllic spot for a picnic or an overnight bivouac.

Lomond has a dock for visiting boats, as well as a launching ramp. With a small boat or canoe, it is fun to explore the various coves and inlets of the arm and the estuary of the Lomond River. In the shallows there are clams and mussels to be found. Bald eagles often can be seen for they nest in the crags above the river.

In winter, when it remains unploughed, the Lomond road is a popular cross-country ski run. The picnic shelters near the camp grounds provide a welcome place for a boil-up.

The road to Lomond is a fine ski run, with glimpses of Killdevil and the Main Arm of Bonne Bay.

Ponds of the Lomond River

Just outside the Park boundary, on the Lomond River, are two very large and scenic ponds, Bonne Bay Big Pond and Bonne Bay Little Pond.

Bonne Bay Big Pond, which you see three times as you approach the Park on Route 430, is an amazing pond. Shaped like a many-armed sea creature, its shore line is eighty miles around. Nowhere is it very wide, and its many bays, arms and inlets provide delightful boating and sandy shores near the road where it is easy to launch. An interesting feature of the pond is an underground river that spews up very close to the road where it crosses a short causeway. In wet seasons a huge flow of water gushes through the culverts there and into the pond. Bonne Bay Big Pond is a popular cabin area and a friendly place in both summer and winter.

The Bonne Bay road, Route 431, runs along the shore of Bonne Bay Little Pond. Surrounded by steep wooded hills, and with beaches at either end for launching, this very beautiful pond is another excellent place to go canoeing. Where the upper Lomond River enters the pond at the east end there is a big sand bar and the main river slides gently through a reed-lined steady behind it. The sand bar is open at both ends, and usually has beaver workings near it. Paddling around it on a peaceful evening is a delight.

Down river and within the Park is an attractive little trout pond called Stuckless Pond. Set in the hills on the east side of the river, the trail to the pond leaves the highway just east of the Lomond turning, crosses the river, and winds its way up the hill. Here, and throughout the valley, wild flowers are prolific, and in some of the wet and shady spots showy lady's slipper orchids may be found.

The Lomond is a well-known and particularly pretty salmon river. It drops more than two hundred feet in the four miles from Bonne Bay Little Pond to the salt water at Lomond.

Burrage's Gulch

One of the loveliest wilderness areas around Bonne Bay is a little-known valley a few miles up Route 430 from the Park's southern boundary near Wiltondale. It is called Burrage's Gulch after one of Bonne Bay's early settlers. With its three rocky peaks on one side, it always reminds me of the famous Three Sisters of Glencoe in Scotland, and before we knew its correct name a friend and I called it The Valley of the Three Sisters.

As Route 430 drops down towards the Main Arm from the high pass in the hills above Wiltondale, you look across Southeast Brook to a wide notch in the hills. This is Burrage's Gulch. Over the notch, a river cascades in white rushes to join the main brook. One by one the Three Sisters peep out from their secluded valley as you pass.

Because of thick vegetation, the valley is almost inaccessible in summer; in winter, however, it is a wonderful outing on snowshoes or nordic skis up the frozen river. As you go up the narrowing valley, the river becomes a steep ravine with marvelous ice formations at the sides and swirling pools in the snow-hollows. Eventually you come out onto the high, rolling Long Range Plateau.

Burrage's Gulch is an interesting example of a hanging valley, its mouth blocked by a rock barrier which the glaciers failed to grind away. It has fine forest cover and is a favourite place for moose and many other animals. On our many trips in there, we have always seen moose, or recent signs of them, and once found ourselves in the midst of a big moose-yard or winter roost. Since moose are very protective of their wintering yards, we lost no time in getting well clear of it before they returned!

It was here also that two moose displayed their marvelous power and speed in deep snow. We had been toiling slowly along on snowshoes when we came upon a cow and her yearling calf. They took off up the frozen river, headed for a very steep but open hillside. With their high-stepping legs pounding like pistons into the belly-deep snow, they were a mile away and over the ridge in just two or three minutes, their movements apparently as effortless as if the ground were bare.

No doubt the gulch was a favourite hunting ground of that early Mr. Burrage, and so his name came to be associated with this lovely valley.

Snowshoeing up the ravine of Burrage's Gulch.

Killdevil

Killdevil is a scree-sided mountain across the Main Arm from Lomond, and has a special place in the heritage of the Bonne Bay people. With its 2100-foot top barely a mile from the salt water, it has always been one of Newfoundland's relatively accessible climbs. From the early days of the lumbering town of Lomond, and later when Killdevil Lodge became a summer camp ground for guides, scouts and church groups, the climb up Killdevil was always the high point of the summer for the more adventurous youngsters.

For the people of Bonne Bay, Killdevil was the venue of an annual family outing, for part of it is covered with partridge berries. A favourite berry in Newfoundland, it has the great advantage of being almost self-preserving. In all the Bonne Bay communities, before the roads were built, there would be a bustle of preparations in September as families got ready for their main berry-picking outing of the year. Into the fishing boat would go tents, blankets, provisions and cooking pots and big barrels in which to collect the partridge berries. They would land at Barachois Brook and set up camp, then everyone, old and young alike, set off, the men with huge buckets and children with little pots and pails, up the steep rocky slopes to their favourite berry patches. Ten or twenty families might be on the mountain on a fine September day in years gone by.

But humans are not the only berry pickers to be found there. Killdevil is often home to a few bears and fall is a season of glut and easy living for them. One fall, as we moved slowly up a steep slope picking blueberries, we noticed two young bears some three hundred yards across the gully we were in, also busy picking. They noticed us too and sat up to look at us. When both parties recognized that the others were just berry pickers, everyone got on with the job, looking up every so often to see what the others were up to. For us, the only concern was that if they had a mother nearby we did not want to get between her and her cubs, but we picked our way to the top of the mountain without seeing any sign of her. After a walk along the level summit enjoying the view of Bonne Bay and the mountains all around, we started down again. The cubs were still guzzling. But this time we were moving downhill quickly so they felt a bit unsure of us and took off over a ridge for safety.

A sequel to this came a few days later when I scanned the rocky side of Killdevil with binoculars from the shore at Lomond. Sure enough, the two cubs were picking berries again, but this time their mother was with them.

Bears will eat far more berries than they can digest and apparently don't bother to chew when the berries are thick. On another part of Killdevil, in an area rich in squash berries and dogberries, we were once mystified by huge conical piles of berries which seemed to have been tipped out of buckets. It was some time before we tumbled to the fact that these were undigested berries that the bears had deposited in their efforts to stuff themselves with all they could hold!

Killdevil, one of Bonne Bay's handsomest mountains, was nearly the cause of the whole idea of a national park in Bonne Bay being abandoned, for the mountain is almost entirely composed of quartzite, or silica. In 1968/69, when the proposal for a national park in this area was being actively negotiated with the Newfoundland government, the government was preoccupied with the need to obtain a supply of cheap silica for the phosphorus plant at Long Harbour, Placentia Bay. Killdevil and its adjacent mountains would provide a most convenient open cast silica mine and the material could be loaded directly into ships of any size in the deep natural harbour of the East Arm.

In the hope of getting both a new national park and a silica mine, the wildest proposals were made which would have excluded the East Arm of Bonne Bay from the Park altogether, and somehow thrust a road through the Long Range Mountains well to the east to circumvent the mine area. Fortunately, it became evident that this idea was incompatible with the development of a park and that the proposed highway would be impossibly expensive. It also emerged that it was the wish of the people of Newfoundland that a national park be established at Bonne Bay to protect their heritage. And so, after a great deal of political debate, the silica mine proposal was abandoned and the planning for the Park commenced.

CHAPTER 3

Down the Bonne Bay Road

The Western Arm

From the time it was first built, the Bonne Bay Road, linking Woody Point to Deer Lake, has been famous for three things: wonderful scenery; lots of wildlife; and very steep hills. The steepest hill led from the bottom of the Western Arm of Bonne Bay up into the hills, climbing nearly a thousand feet in two and a half miles, and became known, appropriately, as 'The Struggle'. The Park rebuilt the road in 1983 and it is no longer the struggle it used to be, but the old name still remains and you still climb those thousand feet in the same distance.

Of the wildlife in the woods, moose, snowshoe hares and squirrels are the ones most likely to be seen from the roads. The moose are impressive animals when seen at close range, but they cause a lot of accidents by coming out of the woods suddenly in daylight, or by standing, blinded by the lights of a car at night, unable to see their way back across the ditches. Black bears and foxes are also fairly common, but are not often seen from the roads.

The Bonne Bay road has always been lined with a burgeoning array of wildflowers. With the rebuilding of the road, many of the colourful drifts of flowers lining the highway disappeared, to be replaced by tidy banks of grass, clover, or bright yellow bird's foot trefoil. But nature soon began to reassert itself and already the old favourites are reappearing: blue vetch, pink fireweed, pearly everlastings, and a legion of others. Majestic and luxuriant are the six foot plants of cow parsnip, whose umbels of white flowers are as big as plates. This plant is known as hemlock in England, a name the early settlers must have used, but over the years the name has become distorted by repetition to "helltrot" which is one of several names by which it is known locally. The dry flower heads remain standing all winter, and after every snowfall are crowned with glistening cones of snow.

Dropping down the Struggle, the shining water of the Western Arm comes into sight. Green, thickly-wooded hills line the shore, while on the skyline is the high plateau of the Tableland with its bare golden rock and snow patches that last all through the summer. Occupying the lowland at the head of the bay is the community of Glenburnie. It is a neat little place with trim fences, bright green grass and many trees among the houses which give the community a cosy and protected look.

One of the first settlers there was a Scot called MacKenzie. He probably gave the place its Scottish name, and his descendants still live there. The mouth of nearby MacKenzie's Brook is the site of one of the Park's many attractive picnic areas, a lovely place with lush grass and trees and a splendid view down the Bay.

Strung out along the Bay for a mile or two is the community of Birchy Head with a tiny settlement called Silverton on the beach below. On the skyline above Birchy Head is one of Newfoundland's sharpest peaks. Known locally as Pickatinnyree, this strange name seems to be another of the old French names around the coasts of Newfoundland that have become anglicised almost beyond recognition. It may have originated with the French settlers on this coast, or even earlier with Captain James Cook who often named the features he saw after faraway places they resembled. No one can be certain, but there seems little doubt that this name must be Pic à Tenerife, and that the hill must resemble the sharp peak of Tenerife in the Canary Islands that some visiting sailor had seen. Although not a major peak, at 1850 feet it has wonderful views, especially over Bonne Bay and the Tableland. Like so many places where there is no hiking trail, it is reached most easily on snowshoes in winter.

Shoal Brook is the next community. Its original houses are clustered around the mouth of the brook itself while those built in later years are spread along the road almost to Birchy Head. The United Church in Shoal Brook, built in 1916, is one of the oldest churches in the area. An earlier church served also as schoolhouse for the then-Methodist congregation.

Alongside the church, winding steeply up the hill, is an old woods trail. This trail leads up into the valley of the Shoal Brook, known as the Southwest Gulch. The valley lies below the steep eastern escarpment of the Tableland and is very scenic. Unfortunately, it is almost inaccessible in summer because of thick groundcover in the valley; it can be reached, however, on skis or snowshoes in winter.

Between Shoal Brook and Winterhouse Brook is a tiny cove with a sandy beach where the caplin roll in every June. Because of the quarrelsome habits of the families that once lived there it used to be known as Hell Cove, but that was long ago. It now has just a summer population of cheerful campers.

Winterhouse Brook is so named because some of the early settlers used to retreat to more sheltered quarters there for the winter. In summer they had simple cabins close to their fishing wharves and sheds. The marine service centre for this part of the coast has recently been built there and provides safe winter storage for fishing vessels and also for a number of yachts. A small fish plant at Winterhouse Brook is mainly in the business of drying and packaging salt cod.

As you approach Woody Point a road branches off up the hill to the left. This road leads to a very special section of Gros Morne National Park and also to the unique fishing village of Trout River. From this junction, you look down onto a community that has often been compared to places on the Italian Lakes, the town of Woody Point.

Woody Point: A Century of Change

Few people who have sailed or driven in to Woody Point have failed to be impressed by its extraordinary beauty. From the road, one looks down onto a point of land lying at the foot of steep forested hills and projecting into the bay at the entrance to the Western Arm. Between the houses, scattered over the low point, stand the tall plumes of the poplar trees. Beyond lies the broad expanse of Bonne Bay, the far shore dotted

Lombardy poplars, seen against the broad expanse of Bonne Bay and the Long Range, give Woody Point its singular beauty.

with the houses of another community (Norris Point), and on the skyline the mountains of the Long Range with Gros Morne distinctively grey in their midst.

Approaching Woody Point by boat the scene is a remarkable one, for behind the town and its green hills stands a rampart of red-gold rock — the Tableland. It is this contrasting backdrop that makes the scenery of the Western Arm unique among all the other beautiful inlets of the Island.

Every visitor wonders how the Lombardy poplar trees, native to southern Europe, came to flourish in this northerly place, and many who have visited the beautiful Italian Lakes are at once reminded of those poplar-studded landscapes. No one knows how they first came to Newfoundland, but the first ones in Bonne Bay were planted around the turn of the century by the magistrate at that time. They have now become a Bonne Bay tradition and, since they are very easy to grow from a cutting, most people have a few on their land, and they withstand the roaring gales of Bonne Bay as well as any other trees.

Walking around the town's circuit of road, and seeing the spacious two-storey houses of an earlier time, the three fine old churches, and the many stores for such a small town, one realizes that the place looks back to a past of considerable substance. The sheltered bay, deep water and good anchorages of Bonne Bay were noted by Captain James Cook in his 1768 survey of the west coast, and the merchant adventurers from the West of England soon saw it as a good location for a centre for the northwest coast fishery.

The first English settlers came around 1800. Soon a Dorset firm placed an agent in Bonne Bay to organize the collection and shipping of fish. And so began an era that lasted until the 1930s during which Bonne Bay was the chief collecting point for all the dried codfish from the northwest coast, supplying fishing gear and every kind of merchandise in exchange. Salt herring and canned lobster were later processed on a big scale as well. The bay became a major trading place, with ships coming, not only from England, but from all the Atlantic seaboard to leave their cargoes of merchandise and fill their deep holds with fish. Photographs of Bonne Bay taken around 1900 show the many trading schooners that were often anchored off Woody Point.

The people of the west coast had little contact with the Colony's capital, St. John's, until well into the twentieth century. Because of their fish trade and the numerous vessels plying back and forth to Halifax, Boston and the eastern seaboard, the people of Bonne Bay were far more familiar with those places than with their own capital city of St. John's. If a young man went out into the world to seek his fortune, he would most likely head for "the Boston States," taking passage on a merchant vessel. If an organ or a bed, a table or a set of chairs was needed, it would most likely be ordered from Boston. In my house, a fine old settle that must be nearly a hundred years old obviously originated there.

The population and the fish trade grew steadily all through the nineteenth century, but of administration, justice, medicine, education or communications there was little beyond what could be provided by visiting Royal Navy ships or by the merchants. The captains of these ships would settle quarrels, marry couples, send the ship's doctor to tend the sick, and even lend boxes of their own books to the people who were struggling to carve out a life for themselves as settlers.

It was the churches, rather than the colonial government who made the first efforts to help the settlers on the northwest coast. The Methodist, Anglican and Roman Catholic churches all sent clergy into the area around the middle of the nineteenth century. The congregations of each tended to group together so that while Woody Point was largely Anglican, Shoal Brook and Curzon Village were mostly Methodist, and the majority of Roman Catholics lived around Bailey's Point and Winterhouse Brook.

The pioneer clergy, with neither funds nor government services to help them, wrought wonders, working entirely alone with their scattered flocks. Indeed, much of the social history of that time is bound up with their work and is recorded in their modest but graphic writings. Those most concerned with Woody Point were the first two Anglican clergymen to be based in Bay of Islands (where Corner Brook is now located), who served the whole section of coast from there to Cow Head. The first to be appointed was a remarkable young man, the Reverend U.Z. Rule, recently out from England. He was to spend seven years there, travelling his vast parish mostly on foot. The Reverend Rule was responsible for getting the first simple churches built by his parishioners in Woody Point and in Cow Head, and in the same buildings he started the first schools. His successor, another extraordinary Englishman, was Reverend J.J. Curling, after whom the first settlement on Bay of Islands was named. He was a well-educated and much-travelled man, a military engineer and an expert sailor. He had his own vessel and an independent income, which he used freely to further his work. Both Reverend Rule and Reverend Curling were supported by their friends in England with funds to help in the building of churches in Newfoundland. Curling designed and built a fine church in Woody Point and its heavy oak doors are still in use in the present Anglican church.

The beautiful Roman Catholic church, St. Patrick's, was originally built on Bailey's Point in 1875. Later it was moved to Woody Point where it still stands, the oldest and the prettiest church in the Catholic diocese.

The education of the settlers' children took high priority with all the denominations, and they lost no time in establishing schools in the communities they served. The Reverend Curling, being an avid reader himself, was concerned too at the plight of the settlers who had no way of obtaining books to further their knowledge or culture. In 1879 he

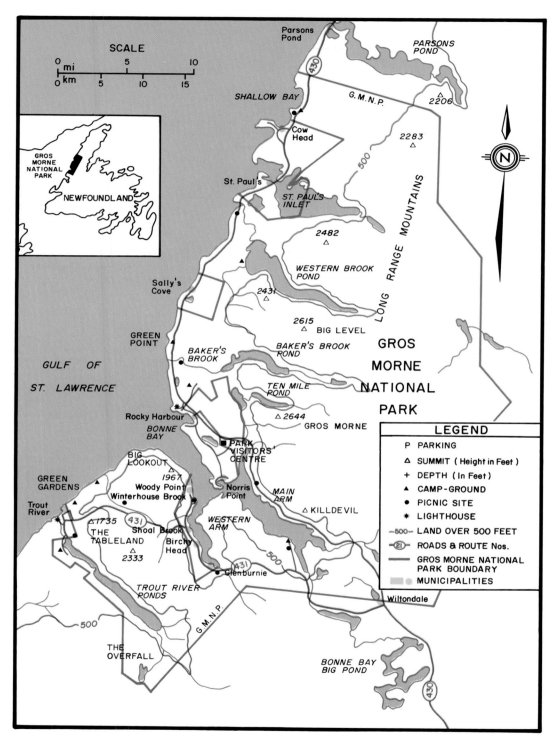

SCALE

0 mi   5   10
0 km 5   10   15

GROS MORNE NATIONAL PARK
NEWFOUNDLAND

Parsons Pond

PARSONS POND

SHALLOW BAY

G.M.N.P.

△ 2206

Cow Head

2283 △

St. Paul's

ST. PAUL'S INLET

500

2482 △

LONG RANGE MOUNTAINS

Sally's Cove

WESTERN BROOK POND

2431 △

GREEN POINT

2615 △ BIG LEVEL

BAKER'S BROOK

BAKER'S BROOK POND

GROS MORNE NATIONAL PARK

GULF OF ST. LAWRENCE

TEN MILE POND

△ 2644

GROS MORNE

Rocky Harbour

BONNE BAY

PARK VISITORS' CENTRE

LEGEND

P PARKING
△ SUMMIT (Height in Feet)
+ DEPTH (In Feet)
▲ CAMP-GROUND
● PICNIC SITE
✳ LIGHTHOUSE
—500— LAND OVER 500 FEET
㉑ ROADS & ROUTE Nos.
——— GROS MORNE NATIONAL PARK BOUNDARY
▨● MUNICIPALITIES

BIG LOOKOUT

GREEN GARDENS

△ 1967

Woody Point
Winterhouse Brook

Norris Point

MAIN ARM

△ KILLDEVIL

Trout River

△ 1735
THE TABLELAND

Shoal Brook

431

Birchy Head

△ 2333

WESTERN ARM

500

TROUT RIVER PONDS

Glenburnie

431

Wiltondale

G.M.N.P.

500

THE OVERFALL

BONNE BAY BIG POND

430

Gros Morne National Park and Environs

25

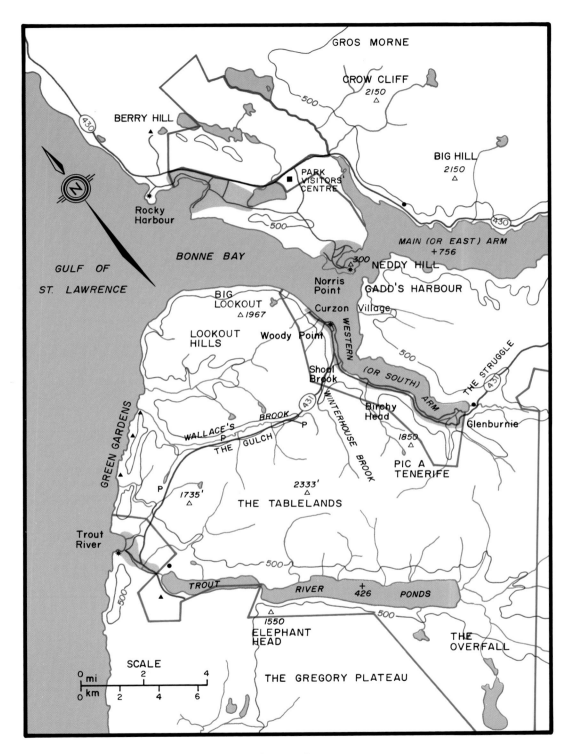

The Southwest

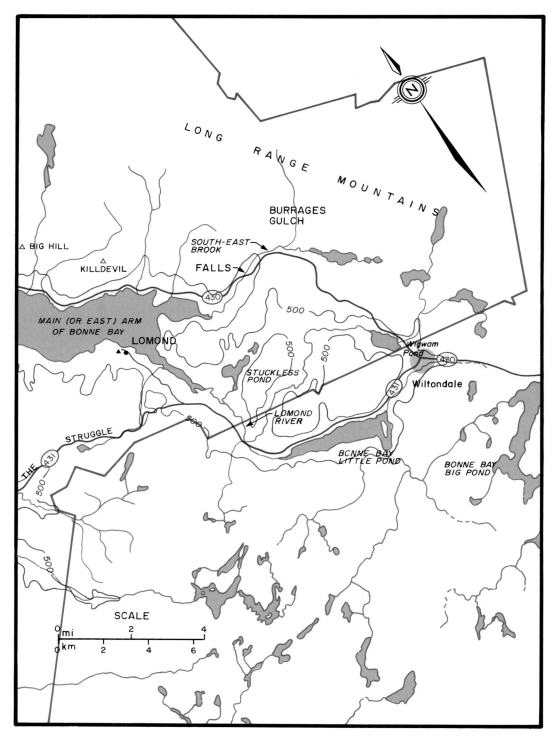

The Southeast

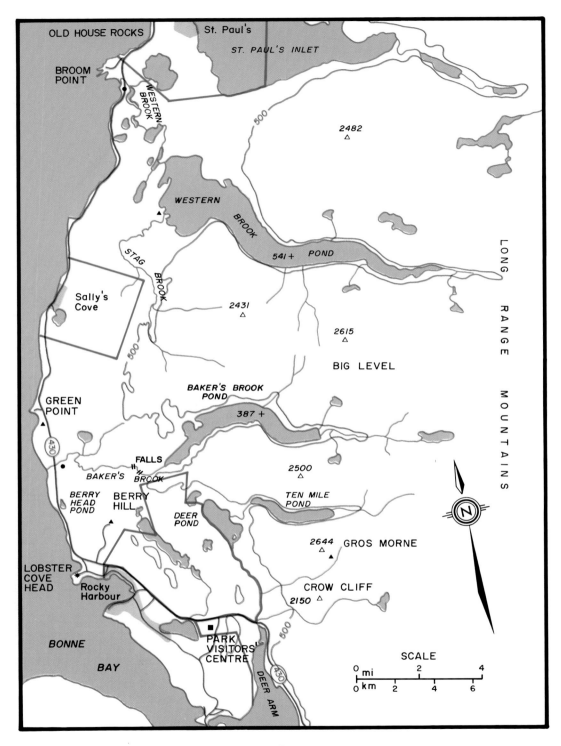

OLD HOUSE ROCKS   St. Paul's

ST. PAUL'S INLET

BROOM POINT

WESTERN BROOK

2482 △

WESTERN BROOK POND

STAG BROOK

541 +

Sally's Cove

2431 △

2615 △

BIG LEVEL

BAKER'S BROOK POND

387 +

GREEN POINT

430

FALLS

BAKER'S BROOK

2500 △

BERRY HEAD POND

BERRY HILL

DEER POND

TEN MILE POND

2644 △

GROS MORNE

LOBSTER COVE HEAD

Rocky Harbour

CROW CLIFF

2150 △

BONNE BAY

PARK VISITORS' CENTRE

430

DEER ARM

LONG RANGE MOUNTAINS

N

SCALE

0 mi   2   4

0 km   2   4   6

The Centre

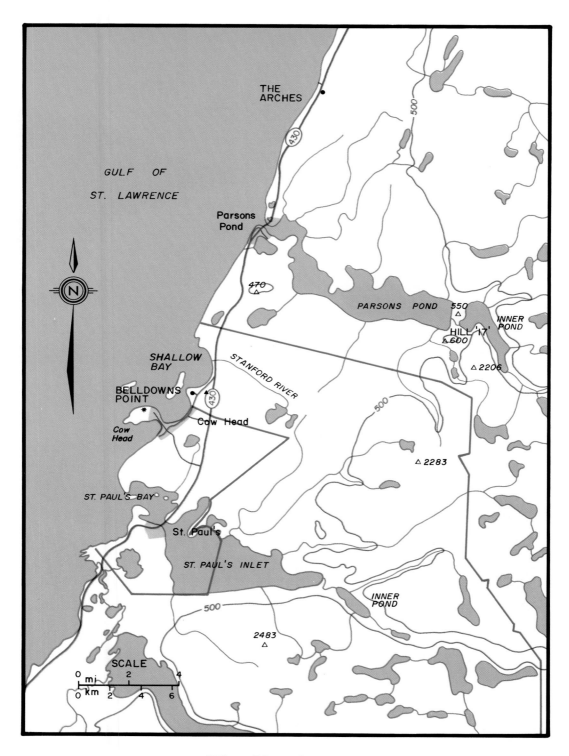

The Northwest

Canoeing up the estuary of the Lomond River.

Showy lady's slipper orchids in the Lomond valley.

Killdevil rewards the climber with marvellous views.

Shoal Brook, one of the pretty communities lining the shore of the Western Arm of Bonne Bay.

Boats hauled out for the winter at the marine service centre at Winterhouse Brook.

Pic à Tenerife.

Woody Point and the Western Arm of Bonne Bay on an early summer morning.

Once a fire-watcher's vantage point, Big Lookout has some of the finest views in the Park.

put together a collection of some three hundred books — his own and many given by friends — and set up a little lending library.

The first medical service grew out of a combination of desperate need and natural talent. Alfred Prebble, a merchant from Maine who traded fish and merchandise in his own vessel, possessed a natural talent for coping with ills and accidents. As more and more problems were brought to him, he began to buy and study medical books. A woman with similar natural skills assisted him, and later became his wife. In 1863 he built a house in Woody Point where he carried on his business, but later moved across to Norris Point. All his life, Alfred Prebble continued to study and practice his self-taught medicine around Bonne Bay, never refusing a sick call. Eventually the Newfoundland government and the medical association of the day recognized his skill and service by giving him the title of Doctor, and an official license to practice. His son was similarly gifted and carried on after his father died until the first fully qualified doctor was appointed in the 1920s.

Toward the end of the century public services at last began to be introduced, first a post office in 1873 and soon afterwards a telegraph office. In the mid-1870s the first political representative was elected, but because of the difficulties of travel he was seldom seen in his district. A magistrate was appointed near the end of the century, and later a courthouse was built in Woody Point. With the establishment of the first regular coastal boat service and the completion of the trans-island railway the last decade of the century proved to be the turning point between the complete isolation of the pioneer years and the network of communications that links Bonne Bay to every other part of the Province today.

The early years of the new century saw a steady improvement in the fortunes of the Bonne Bay area and by the 1920s Woody Point had reached the peak of its prosperity as a centre for trade. The town had also become the administrative base for the northwest coast, with the courthouse, customs house, welfare officer, and the police (then the Newfoundland Ranger Force) all located at Woody Point. But at this point disaster struck.

A fire, fanned by high winds, swept through all the major business premises and homes on the waterfront. As the whole northwest coast was dependent upon these stores for fishing gear and provisions of every kind, it was a disaster that affected everyone living there, a disaster that was compounded by the onset of the Depression in 1929. Woody Point never recovered from the blow.

The life of the fisherman became even harder in the Depression years. Supplied with fishing gear and provisions on credit, to be paid for in saltfish at the end of the season, the fisherman lived in almost permanent debt to the merchant. This combination of credit and barter was known as the "truck system" and under it the fisherman was lucky if he received even a small payment in hard cash at the end of the season. When the economy collapsed, he got almost nothing for his catch and had to look to the merchant for his very survival. With the modernization of the fishing industry in later years, the truck system gradually came to an end.

The Second World War, with all its grief and horror, was to bring relief from the desperate problems left by the Depression. The need for military construction brought a rush of jobs, and when men were needed to work in the forests of Scotland many from Bonne Bay went over. In joining up in the armed forces, as so many did, a man was thankful to be able to secure a steady income for his family, albeit at the hazard of his life. In short, the war introduced a cash economy to Newfoundland for the first time.

It also brought far-reaching technical advances. Radio not only brought news of the war and the world into the community, it was the start of the technology that was eventually to bring an element of safety into the hazardous job of fishing. With radionavigation beacons and ready communication between boats and shore, and later all the refinements of radar and sonar, radio was to revolutionize the life of the fisherman.

Confederation with Canada in 1949 brought added security, and benefits of every kind to the community. The development of the new Province's road system during the 1950s and '60s made tourism a factor in Newfoundland, and for many years Woody Point seemed to have a promising future as a tourist resort. All traffic heading up the Great Northern Peninsula came through Woody Point and across the Bonne Bay ferry. "Beautiful Bonne Bay" became a byword, both in Newfoundland and beyond, and people came from far and wide to see it.

The building of the northern peninsula highway and the beginning of work on the new national park brought welcome employment, but, with the establishment of the Park in the early 1970s, it soon became apparent that the hub of the local economy would shift to Rocky Harbour and with it would go the role of administrative centre for the area, a position so long held by Woody Point. The drift began very soon with the police, and later the bank, moving across the bay.

Gros Morne, having given its name to the new park, is now its focal point, and with the new Route 430 along the shore of the East Arm leading directly to the Park's main facilities at Rocky Harbour, traffic naturally follows the northward road through Wiltondale. The south side of Bonne Bay, the part referred to as "Beautiful Bonne Bay," is now easily bypassed by many visitors to the region.

The ferry that used to link Woody Point to Norris Point ceased operation in 1985, so these two closely related communities are now more than an hour's drive apart. The economy of both places owed much to the ferry link which was regarded as part of the local road system.

It is often said that the Bonne Bay ferry trip was the most scenic one east of British Columbia. With the added glimpses of marine life to be seen on the way, the twenty-minute crossing has been for many visitors the highlight of their whole journey through Newfoundland. For the sake of the thousands of people who come to visit Gros Morne National Park every year, one hopes that the Bonne Bay ferry soon will be in operation again.

Woody Point, whose whole history has been one of change, for better and for worse, is still adjusting to the momentous changes of the last fifteen years and seeking its new role in the life of the area.

Big Lookout

For many years the fire lookout for all the forest areas around Bonne Bay, Big Lookout commands a wide circle of views, and those views that made it such a good fire lookout now reward the hiker who climbs it. Since the coming of the Park the whole section of hills that lie between Trout River Gulch and the mouth of Bonne Bay have come to be known as the Lookout Hills.

Big Lookout is, roughly speaking, a thousand foot peak on a thousand foot plateau. In actual fact it is 1967 feet, and this prompted one of the first Park interpreters to nickname it Centennial Peak. Since then, however, we've gone metric, but who wants to change the name that it has had for a hundred years and more?

The old fire-watcher's trail goes straight up from Woody Point, starting just below the water tower where you cross Crolly's Brook. It is quite steep, and like a lot of natural Newfoundland trails which tend to become water courses, it is wet underfoot. The small trees on the steep slope include a lot of red maple, along with birch, spruce and fir, so the hillside is a wonderful mix of colours in the fall. Early in the summer the pink moccasin orchid grows all along these hillsides, as does the trailing arbutus — mayflower to Newfoundlanders.

As you climb, the trees thin out and gradually you come into the open to a fine view of Woody Point and the bay. Soon, as you follow the shallow valley, Big Lookout comes into view about three miles away. The ground is boggy and wet much of the way, but full of interesting plants. Pitcher plants are numerous, and their tiny fellow-carnivorous plant, the sundew, makes a dewy pink mat in the muddy hollows with its sticky little paddle-like leaves. Brilliant patches of yellow bladderwort sometimes share these wet spots. Sheep laurel and the similar bog laurel (kalmia) both have the same exquisite pink parachute-like flowers and are among the prettiest of the flowering shrubs. Other shrubs forming much of the groundcover are Labrador tea with its white flower heads and suede-backed leaves, pink-flowered rhodora, blueberry, and the sweet-scented bog myrtle.

This mixture of shrubs, together with wind-dwarfed spruce, although hard to walk through is ideal cover, and also the feeding place for willow ptarmigan. Having sat still until you are too close for comfort, the ptarmigan fly up with a great cackle. In summer they are likely to have chicks hiding nearby, and to divert your attention they will sometimes make a very obvious and clumsy landing close by. If you follow them they fly a little further, and so gradually draw you away and leave their chicks in safety.

It is not unusual to see one or two caribou up on this rolling high ground. They travel over from the Gregory Plateau that lies just south of the Park, making their way alongside the Tableland through the Southwest Gulch. On the high, rocky areas of the Lookout Hills there are plenty of patches of the grey-white caribou moss on which they feed. You may at least see their foot prints (which are like moose prints, only smaller) and their droppings (which look very like those of sheep, but there are no sheep up there).

The path to the top of Big Lookout goes along the foot of the hill at first, and where a clump of spruce and fir stand in a hollow, the path turns sharply right and dips down through the trees before starting up the steep rocky slope. The top of Big Lookout is a rocky crag, the highest of several small peaks that look as though a rough cone had split apart. From the steep ridge and cliff that lead to the summit, you look down into the green hollow that separates them. With this cliff in the foreground, there is a spectacular view back over Bonne Bay. Soon you are on the top, and from there, on a clear day, you can see as far as Portland Hill, nearly fifty miles to the north. Rocky Harbour is a neat horseshoe across the mouth of the bay, and Gros Morne, some twelve miles away, looks most impressive from this angle.

Big Lookout is a very rewarding hike from Woody Point, taking about two and a half hours to climb up, and less to come down. But, as much of the route is wet and boggy, one must either wear rubber boots or not mind wet feet.

Apart from the old fire-watcher's trail, it is almost impossible to walk on the plateau in summer due to the knee-high or hip-high groundcover and the tuckamore in the hollows. In winter, however, once there is plenty of snow, you can go just about anywhere on the plateau using snowshoes. Some of our favourite winter hikes have been out along the top of the bluffs lining the entrance to Bonne Bay, passing between Big Lookout and the bay and going on out to Western Head. The terrain is magnificent. The cliffs are layered and patterned where extensive rock faces have slipped many years ago. Thick forests cover the bluffs, and above the trees stand the rock pinacles known as the Old Man and his Sons, so conspicuous when seen from the water. Seen at close quarters, the Old Man is the size of a three-storey house.

High in these impenetrable woods, a pair of bald eagles often nest.

CHAPTER 4

The Cove

Curzon Village

Curzon Village is an odd-sounding name for Newfoundland, where the word village is hardly ever used. It has, somehow, stuck in this instance. The name comes from a Commander Curzon of the Royal Navy who sailed his patrol vessel into Bonne Bay early in the nineteenth century.

Curzon Village is more often referred to locally as The Cove (meaning Crolly's or, more correctly, Crawley's Cove), which is the area around the mouth of Crolly's Brook. It is here that the majority of the fishermen have their sheds and wharves and where now a community wharf gives shelter to a couple of longliners. But it is still called The Cove, right down to the last house, half a mile away.

In its early days, Curzon Village was almost entirely a fishing community. The houses, in comparison to those of the prosperous merchants of Woody Point, were small and humble. The story goes that a British naval officer, sailing close to the shore of Curzon Village, remarked to a fellow officer, "Those are fine geese-houses I see by the shore there!" This was in 1874. My house was built the year before and was no doubt one of them!

Although Curzon Village seems to be just an extension of Woody Point toward the mouth of the bay, it has quite a distinct character. One major difference, very significant in years gone by, was that most of the people of Curzon Village were Methodist. The denominations tended to keep to their own, and each had its own school as well as church. With the changes in lifestyle and the universal move toward ecumenicism, these differences have faded. Now the Anglican and United Church congregations are quite comfortable in each other's churches on special occasions, and few could clearly explain the differences between the two. It is mainly family tradition that keeps people in their accustomed church.

In years gone by there were many more houses beyond the present end of the community; several have been hauled closer to Woody Point. In this age of paved roads and permits, this is now seldom done, but over the years, when somebody wanted to move his house it was just shifted onto big wooden skids and hauled by every available

Curzon Village, Woody Point, and the Western Arm photographed from the hills above the author's house.

man, woman, child, horse and dog to its new location — an event enjoyed by all, and always an excuse for a celebration.

During my time there have been two major house-haulings in Curzon Village. One involved a house in Glenburnie at the foot of the bay. It was hauled down to the shore and its lower rooms filled with empty oil drums, braced in position with lumber. It was then pushed off into the water and taken in tow by the ferry boat for the six-mile voyage to Curzon Village. It took up a position with one sill as keel and sailed majestically along in this fashion. This being the age of the bulldozer, three big ones hauled the house up the steep slope to its chosen site. I think everyone in the community turned out for that event, and felt quite at a loss with no ropes to haul!

Another sensational hauling made use of heavy ice on the bay one very cold winter. A large fish shed, two storeys high, was moved from the shore below my house at the end of Curzon Village to a spot further in the bay. Two pickup trucks took it in tow, their wheels spinning as they struggled to move its immense weight. Eventually it got going and the procession took off at surprising speed — too much speed as it turned out, for momentum kept the shed going on the shining ice while the two trucks, unable to stop it, were slewed around and towed along backwards! Finally, with all hands and several snowmobiles to help, the big shed reached the appointed spot on the beach and stayed there till spring, when it was jacked up on shores and settled into place.

Crossing the mouth of Bonne Bay on the ice, the shortest and safest route runs from the end of Curzon Village to the low neck of the peninsula in Norris Point, a distance of about two and a half miles. Not all that long ago, in the days when the mail was carried across either by boat or dogteam, the worst times of the year for the mailmen were during freeze-up and break-up. They waited impatiently for either bearing ice or open water. Skilled and daring as they were, they took appalling risks and many of them became legends in their own lifetimes in their determination to get the mail through without delay.

One oldtimer, now in his eighties, was famous for crossing the bay on the merest skin of ice. To lessen the risks, he would lash a small dory on top of his sled so that if they broke through the ice he could scramble in, haul the dogs aboard, and row to the next bearing ice, and so out and on again. A middle-aged woman in Woody Point vividly remembers crossing the bay in this fashion, safely tucked into the dory, to have her baby at the hospital in Norris Point.

The mail carriers were among the toughest men imaginable. When the snow was deep and soft they would run on snowshoes for mile after mile, ahead of the dogs, to make a track for them.

Dogteams were the main winter transportation, and nearly every family had its team of five or ten dogs. They were a motley breed, just big and strong, and only a few, imported from Labrador, had husky blood in their veins. Due to the hard life they led, the dogs were often ill-tempered and dangerous. People had a hearty respect for them, and many still instinctively fear any large dog. All the communities must have had a considerable population of dogs and the older people talk nostalgically of the music of their howling.

Just as nearly every family had its dogteam, and a pony or two for hauling logs in the woods, so now they have snowmobiles. When the ice in the bay is well established it becomes a highway in all directions, with people visiting friends across the bay, youngsters racing their snowmobiles, and men buzzing back and forth towing loads of logs for fuel and lumber. If the ice is clear there will be skating and hockey games on the smooth patches. When it is snow-covered, which is most of the time, the ice gives the area a whole new dimension for hiking and cross-country skiing, and opens up places normally only accessible by boat.

Once the snow is gone, Gros Morne's wilderness areas become well nigh impenetrable for most of us, except where there are Park or woods trails. But talking with some of the older men among my neighbours, I have come to realize what enormous distances they covered on foot in the old days in order to go lumbering or hunting. There is no part of the terrain they don't know, and the paths they used to travel could only be learned by experience. They are unrecognizable as paths to any outsider, but they lead everywhere.

To watch a couple of Newfoundland men set off through the country to go fishing or hunting is to realize what they mean when they use the word "travelling" in its old sense. They strike out with a gait quite different from any you would see them use around home. It is a distinctive, fast, direct, long stride which seems to disregard obstacles and scrub. They don't even seem to have to look where they are going, for their eyes are always scanning around with the instinctive hunter's glance that will pick up the least sign of an animal that most of us would never see. They travel over the roughest ground at the speed of a fast hiker on a good trail and are out of sight in no time. Having bush-whacked through much of Gros Morne before the Park built trails, this phenomenal inbred ability never fails to impress me. When they use the word "travelling" in the context of the woods and mountains, this is what they mean.

Just as the word travelling has an old and a new meaning, so too has the word "cruising." In times past, "going cruising" referred to those rare occasions when the fishing boat could be spared from its daily work to give the family a treat. The fisherman and his family might take a few days to visit friends along the coast, or spend a day in some favourite little cove, the highlight of which would be a good scoff and a boil-up. Now that cars and pickups have taken the place of the boat for most family outings, grandfather will tell you, with a twinkle in his eye as they take off, "We're goin' crusin'!"

Old House by the Shore

Eighteen hundred and seventy — that's about the time the great white pines were cut on the sloping land by Tuff's Brook at the end of Curzon Village.

Albert Tuff, lately moved from Ochre Pit Cove on Conception Bay to the west coast in search of better fishing, was getting ready to build his house. Many of the pines he cut were more than two feet in diameter. With a two-man pitsaw they were sawn into the inch boards that were to form the floors and walls and ceilings of the house. The joists and sills and studs were chopped with an adze.

Albert, his wife, and young family — of whom there would eventually be eight — probably lived in a small cabin while he built the house. All the time he was building, he still had to go fishing, and find time to hunt and get his firewood too, so that, from cutting the first tree to driving the last square-cut nail, the construction must have taken him three or four years. As the last siding was put on he must have had a little good luck ceremony for, laid among the wood shavings that insulated the south wall, he placed a small carved figure, very similar to the charm figures of much more ancient cultures. The tradition may have come with him from his native Dorset.

He built well, for one hundred and ten years later the house still stands, and little of his original pine construction has had to be renewed. His son, Jabez, inherited the house and lived to a ripe old age. Jabez and his wife were a close couple, and Annie was much loved by everyone. But she was so badly crippled by arthritis that she could scarcely leave the house. When she couldn't see what her husband was doing outside, her neighbours would hear her familiar cry from the window, "Wass you up to now Jabe?"

Long after Annie died, in a quiet ceremony held in the parlour, Jabez married again. The Methodist minister, who had long been their boarder, officiated. Jabez' cousin, Roland, and his wife (who was also named Annie) witnessed the wedding. The daguerreotype photographs of Jabez and Annie gazed down from the wall. As Jabez placed the ring on his wife's finger, Roland's Annie looked up at them and, in her mind, heard her old neighbour say once again, "Wass you up to now Jabe?"

For many years after Jabez' death the old house stood empty. In 1968, with flaking paint, it basked in the sun of a blazing June day, surrounded only by a few sheep and close-nibbled grass.

A friend and I, with several weeks of freedom ahead of us before buckling down to new jobs on the mainland, had pitched our tent just beyond the house beside the rushing brook. We had planned a leisurely summer, sailing, hiking and exploring in the Bonne Bay area, then still several years away from becoming a national park. It was part of our plan to rent a cabin or a small house and when we found that we could rent this old house at the end of Curzon Village, only fifty feet from the shore, we were delighted. There were no creature comforts, but it was great to have a roof over our heads instead of a tent and to have room to dry the wet clothes that go with sailing and hiking.

From the outside it had much charm, but once inside, looking out from its windows at the views on every side, we were completely enchanted by it. Not only its outlook, but the gracious proportions of its rooms, the wide staircase, and the bedrooms under the sloping roof where the window sills were just knee-high all combined to make it one of the most charming little houses we had ever seen.

As we were both reluctant to leave Newfoundland, the chance to acquire such an ideal pied-a-terre to come back to for holidays seemed too good to miss, and when the owner agreed to sell for a price we could afford, we made a rapid decision to take a year off in which to fix it up. Working from dawn to dusk, we lived like church mice off our savings. With the help of a local carpenter and plumber, we got through the

39

main repair jobs and had it weather-tight and plumbed before winter struck. It was a great day when the wiring, which we did ourselves, passed inspection and the first switch was thrown.

That busy back-breaking year had many compensations. We soon got to know our neighbours and made friends around the village. Their hospitality and generosity knew no bounds. One family lent us their spare chairs and beds; another an oil heater and a lamp or two. A brand new rocking chair was delivered, complete with a welcoming party, by a group of our new friends. We would often find a fat codfish by the door in the morning, a gift from the old fisherman whose wharf was nearby.

Seeing us two "townies" — and females at that — struggling with the restoration work, they were full of practical advice and gave us all kinds of help. We soon realized that "the cottage," as it was known, was everybody's favourite old house and we had lots of visitors, intrigued to see what we were doing. We felt they were quite glad to see that the old house was getting a new lease on life. And so, as they involved themselves in our efforts to restore the old cottage, we in turn became involved in village life and tried to bend our experiences of life to make ourselves useful in this new context of a small rural community.

The old house by the shore.

Our interests were many and various, but one that we shared with our new friends and neighbours was an interest in crafts and in seeing craft skills revived and developed as a possible source of income for people in the area. Plans for the new national park were taking shape and seemed likely to materialize. The park would bring many visitors, and there would soon be a demand for good local crafts. In meetings and discussions, the idea of a craft shop arose, to provide an outlet for local skills. Many wanted to produce and sell, but no one wanted to have to run the operation.

In the meantime, our year off had come to an end, but the work on the house seemed endless. We were captivated by our surroundings and became involved in many aspects of local affairs. Even less than before did we feel like returning to the daily round of nine-to-five jobs. So, rather than see the craft shop idea shelved, we agreed to set it up on a shoe-string budget and run it for an experimental year. It met with surprising success, and both our producers and our customers encouraged us to continue. A well-placed building became available and it seemed that we had found a niche in the local economy that no one else wanted to fill, and which would benefit a lot of local residents as well as crafts producers from all over the Island. Besides, it enabled us to stay in this wonderful place! And so Bonne Bay Crafts began, developed, and continued for all of fifteen years.

The establishment of Bonne Bay Crafts led also to the setting up of Bonne Bay Weavers, a community weaving studio which runs courses and workshops. People from both sides of the bay use the weavery's six looms, and many weavers who learned their craft in Bonne Bay are now scattered across Canada.

Thus the craft shop and the weavery, and our own craft production, came to dominate our lives. But these activities were always balanced by the time we managed to spend exploring, observing and learning in the magnificent terrain by which we were surrounded. Quite rapidly we learned in the first years that nature, the climate and the weather are the factors that really count when you live in the country and fairly close to the earth. They set the deadlines and dictate what must be done.

The day of the year that is, for me, the beginning of the cycle, the thrust that sets the year in motion, is the day of the winter solstice. On that day, the first beam of the late-rising sun from far in the southeast shafts horizontally through the house to light up an old door, far at the back of the kitchen. In this old house that shaft of brilliant light in the dark corner signals for me the start of nature's new year. Christmas is but a day or two away, but deeply underlying the celebration of the birth of Christ are ancient stirrings of the blood that man has known since first he recognized that mid-winter's darkness is but a new beginning. The urge to celebrate the turn of the year is something buried deep in our bodies, beyond consciousness or thought. It is part of that same mystery that drives the birds to migrate and the sap to rise.

Far from dreading the coming months of winter, one looks forward with a certain relish to the days when the house shakes in the wind and snow batters the windows, while inside all is snug and the well-fed woodstove blazes. The first real snowstorm is something we enjoy. With morning, all the world seems created anew, all man's untidiness buried under a sparkling blanket of snow.

Swirling like snow flurries come the first flocks of snow buntings, driven southward by the advancing winter. They cheer the bleakest day with their wild, wheeling flight and happy chattering.

The day the ice catches over begins the season of quietness, with no waves beating on the shore, no white-caps, and no roar of wind over water. It is suddenly not so much a different season as a different world. Ice two or three feet thick only occurs every few years, but most winters the bay freezes over around the end of January. The process of sea-ice freezing during a cold spell is fascinating to watch. First the water gets cold enough for fallen snow to stay suspended in the water, then it starts to form tiny pans, the size of saucers, near the shore. Soon they are the size of soup plates, and in a couple of days as big as dining room tables. At that point a particularly cold still night usually fills the gaps and it all skins over, the table tops whiter than the new ice in between. Suddenly you can't just glance out and see which way the wind is blowing. There are no waves to tell you, so you must go out and feel the wind on your cheek.

41

Watching the ice on the shore below the house, the rise and fall of the tide shows the extraordinary capacity of sea ice to bend under pressure. Twice every day, as well as cracking, it bends and curves to meet the four foot change in the level of the main ice sheet. Sometimes one hears a crack or a creak, but mostly it is such a silent and imperceptible process that it is hard to believe that the tides are still changing!

As winter passes there comes a day, or a week, in early spring when the wind suddenly blows southerly, bringing balmy air and jolting the plant world into the growing season. A subtle change comes over the woods; the birches have somehow acquired a rich purple look as their buds have begun to swell; the stems of the red osier dogwood are so red they look like lobster antennae sticking up through the snow. All around Bonne Bay it is time to look for mayflowers, the pale pink trailing arbutus that emerges from the snow in bud. After a day or two in water, they burst into flower and fill the house with their sweet scent.

On a warm, calm evening in early May — or even after dark — one hears the first snipe drumming as he courts his new mate above the bogs on the ridge behind us. It is a clear, soft, magical sound that he makes with his wings as he drops from high in the air. No sound heralds the spring as does that reedy trill. The spring bird migration is a time of welcoming old friends, but among them there are sometimes strangers — one year a shrike, another a bobolink, and yet another three Baltimore orioles.

June is a month when everything has to be done at once: the winter's craft productions have to be finished and the shop needs fitting up for the season. At the same time, the weeds are trying to swamp the seedling plants in the garden and the greenhouse needs constant attention. In the midst of it all comes the annual caplin scull, that orgy of reproductive activity that brings the little fish swarming into every sandy cove. There's no time to lose, for in a few days they'll be gone. So we drop everything, gather waders, nets and buckets, and make for Hell Cove or Trout River to dip up enough for fertilizer for the garden and a good supply for the freezer. The milestones of early summer for us gardeners are the days of first harvesting, the first delicious rhubarb and, by the beginning of July, the first young lettuces.

Sometime nearly every summer there will be a day of "Bonne Bay sky" — a day when heavy overcast gradually forms clouds that look as solid as concrete, shaped into such smooth and beautiful contours that a whole army of sculptors must surely have formed them. It may last minutes, or hours, and is a phenomenon I have seen nowhere else and must have to do with the particular draughts and funnellings caused by the surrounding hills.

At summer's height comes a day, or rather a night, when we become aware of the plankton that is in the bay. Every stroke of an arm or a canoe paddle rouses these tiny creatures to sparkling luminescence. Those you stir up in a tidal pool light up to show their beautiful minute patterns as you hold them in the palm of your hand. With all our visitors, a night paddle on the bay is an experience they will never forget, and not only because of the phosphorescence glinting in the wake of the boat. If the moon is full, it rises almost opposite the house. Paddling or rowing on the calm night water, the shimmering moon-path and the moon-lit mountains fill one's soul and the rest of the world ceases to exist.

Late summer sees a great harvesting of fruits and vegetables, just reward for all the work and kelp and slug-bait that went into their production. We have our share of insect pests, but along with the cabbage-white butterflies whose catepillars devour our greens, come some of the loveliest butterflies I have ever seen. They appear in great numbers, among them splendid black and yellow swallow-tails, elegant mourning cloaks, red admirals, tiny blues and painted ladies.

With a clatter of their double wings, the big handsome dragonflies come cruising in. Despite their iridescent green eyes and generally fearsome appearance, they seem to do no harm at all, and I have yet to discover what they eat or prey on. Millions of years ago, when they were apparently about two feet long, they must have been formidable creatures!

One summer a fast-flying creature hovered over the flowers so like a hummingbird that I thought it was one. But when its rapid wing beat was stilled, it turned out to be a hummingbird moth, so big and heavy that I wondered how its small transparent wings could keep it airborne. Hummingbirds, surprisingly, do occur on this coast, and we have twice seen the ruby-throated variety in the garden, attracted by the honeysuckle and the mass of scarlet flowers on our runner beans.

Soon the little yard became a burgeoning garden where flowers and vegetables competed for space.

Probably because the house was for so long empty and provided shelter for those who could creep through crevices, some small animals have come boldly in despite our presence. We had just had a new porch built when Cocoa, the poodle, discovered that we had a lodger underneath it. With growls and barks on one side and furious chitterings on the other, they roundly cussed one another. The lodger was a mink. We had seen his tracks in winter by the brook and glimpsed his small black head swimming by the shore. We drove him out, but a little later he was back to try the main crawl-space underneath the house. This time he had a cod's head, bigger than himself, and was trying to force it through a small hole. Fascinated, we watched as he tried all ways to stow his treasure, aware of us but unconcerned. Finally he abandoned the effort, and the cod's head, and went to look for another lair.

One winter the quietness of the night was suddenly disturbed by heavy pattering in the attic. "Rats!" we thought, and banged on the walls and ceilings to frighten them away. We baited the rat-trap, pushed it through the hatch into the roof-space, and retired to await developments. The pattering soon returned, followed very shortly by the loud snap of the trap. Cocoa flew to the hatch door. As we opened the door and looked in, the flashlight beam fell on the brilliant white, slim body of a weasel, an ermine in his winter coat. As I reached in to remove it, I saw a second weasel making for the trapped one, just a few feet from me. I withdrew in some haste, as did all three of us, Cocoa quickest of all!

Back with big leather mitts and a stick with which to defend myself from this fierce little animal, I returned to get the trap. The weasel was already struggling to drag its trapped chum or mate away and I had to fend him off. As we had no wish to kill weasels, but only to keep rats away, we hoped he would leave of his own accord. And so he did. Seen at those close quarters, they were the most beautiful little creatures and we were sorry to have inadvertently killed one of them. However, we did not want them as lodgers!

The other fine animals of that family that we have seen close to the house are otters. They have a lair a mile along the seaward shore which they use from time to time, and we had seen chewed bits of fish and lobster on the ice close by. Later in the winter when the ice was breaking up and there was a pool of open water at the mouth of Tuff's Brook, we watched one fishing, not fifty yards from the window. He came up with a wriggling flounder, chomped a few good bites out of it, cleaned his whiskers, and went off to look for something else. Another winter we watched an otter travel over broken ice the full width of the bay from Gadd's Harbour, his dark coat very conspicuous as he alternately loped and swam across.

One morning the dog roused us, having heard something on the road in front of the house. Luckily we didn't let him out to investigate, and for the next half hour we were able to watch a chasing game between the neighbours' small brown dog and a young red fox cub. The dog chased the fox as far as our house, where they both sat down; then the cub chased the dog back to his house. And so it went on till both were tired and the fox cub went on his way.

But of all the fascinating goings-on we have seen from the windows of this old house the most vivid in my mind took place on another very early summer morning, just across the brook. A litter of four silver fox cubs, about half grown, were having a wild romp. Their slim bodies flew like feathers as they leapt in the air, twisted and turned, jumped over each other and onto each other. They seemed to have no weight at all as they bounded and rolled, wrestled and ran in wild circles. Suddenly they were all exhausted and flopped down. A few minutes later they trotted quickly away, up the hill. Whenever I think of them I can see the whole wild game again in my mind.

This old house by the shore has rewarded us with a remarkable store of sights and discoveries. It has also, of course, been the base of operations for all the trips and experiences described in the course of this book.

CHAPTER 5

A World of Ice and Water

Bonne Bay

This deep double fjord has been used by mariners since time immemorial as one of the few safe harbours on a long and savage coast. We know from old maps that, over the centuries, it has had several names. On a seventeenth century map its distinctive shape appears as Dead Man's Bay; a later French one shows it as La Belle Baie. The present, partly French name of Bonne Bay seems to have been used for at least a couple of hundred years. The Maritime Archaic Indians and Dorset Eskimos who lived along its shores over a span of thousands of years must have had their own names for it.

At the present time each of the two arms of Bonne Bay is known by two names, the ones used on the maps and those used by the residents of the area. Captain Cook, surveying the coast and naming the main features in the eighteenth century, called them the East and the South Arm. The Park and the topographical maps use these names, but the two Arms are always known by the people who live beside them as the Main and the Western Arm. So, since both forms are correct, I have used either, depending on the context, with a slight preference for the local names since these are the ones I learned from my neighbours when I became a *livyer* myself.

Apart from its unique scenery, Bonne Bay has the distinction of being deeper than any water in the Gulf of St. Lawrence, with a depth of 756 feet off Norris Cove on the Main Arm. Its great depth and the heavy tide that races through the Tickle at Norris Point, bearing a flood of food and sediment, may be the reason it attracts all manner of sea creatures from minute plankton to the great whales. Marine biologists find it a special place to study, and Memorial University of Newfoundland has a research unit at Norris Point, a busy place at any time of year with scientists studying the waters of the bay and the rich life within them.

Living so close to the water for so many years I have become at least somewhat aware of the teeming life that goes on beneath the surface and recognize the bay as a fascinating but little understood world of its own.

The Ice Edge

In April, after the icebreaker has come and gone and the broken ice has drifted out with the tide, an ice edge often remains. It is immediately busy with wildlife.

The bald eagles, absent while the bay is frozen over, miraculously reappear. One sees them quickly, not only because they are so much larger than other birds, but because they are always the object of mobbing by crows, ravens and the bolder gulls who have also just returned to the bay. The eagles sit together by the hour, seldom left in peace, but with the natural dignity of the invulnerable, waiting for one of the others to drop something. They seem to be very lazy about hunting for themselves.

One unforgettable April day the ice edge ran straight across the mouth of the Western Arm from the ferry dock at Woody Point. The Bonne Bay Weavery, where we were working, was just in line with it so we could see all the activity going on there. We had a pair of binoculars with us, mainly to watch the eagles.

Suddenly we heard and saw a terrific blow of a whale, which hung in a tree-sized cloud as an immense blue-grey back slid through the water. Minutes seemed to pass — actually only a few seconds — before a surprisingly small dorsal fin appeared, followed very shortly as the whale sounded by the biggest flukes we had ever seen. Neither of us had seen a blue whale before, but we knew what they looked like and knew their incredible length to be eighty to one hundred feet. This creature was not only the size of the town's largest building, it was only a couple of hundred yards offshore. Soon we realized there were two of them in close company. Work forgotten, we spent most of that day watching them. They stayed close to the ice edge most of the time, diving repeatedly under it, one usually staying in the open while the other dived.

We went out onto the dock for a better view, and to hear the almost unbelievable power and speed of the blow and inhalation which both take place in the split second that the blow-holes are on the surface. There were so many crowding impressions: their vast and total self-sufficiency; an overwhelming sense of the time span in which these marvelous creatures have evolved over the millennia, moving from the sea, to the land, and back to the sea again, there to become this tremendous tonnage of superbly controlled and graceful motion. They were so close that, with binoculars, one could see a great deal of detail: skin texture, blow-hole, an eye — huge by any normal standard but dwarfed by their enormous bodies. Perhaps the strongest impression was that, with all their size and strength, they posed no threat, emanated no aggression, and seemed entirely benign — except perhaps from the point of view of the tiny creatures they were feeding on!

When sated with food they would spend long periods of time just resting on the surface, companionably parallel and quite close together. At that season all boats are up on land, but had I been able to, I would have borrowed one and happily sat quite close to them on the water, without fear that they would upset a boat either by mistake or on purpose.

They were still around at dusk when we went home, not expecting to see them again, but the feed under that ice edge must have been rich indeed for they stayed most of two weeks. By the time they left for the open sea, they had become familiar to everyone in the village and were regarded as old friends.

Of Whales, Dolphins, Tuna and Seals

There was a time in the early 1970s when there was exceptionally heavy fishing of caplin off the shores of Newfoundland. In addition to the usual inshore caplin fishery, foreign factory ships were allowed very large quotas. As it turned out, these quotas must have been too large for the caplin stocks became badly depleted, and since caplin are some of the main feed of the cod, on which Newfoundland's fishery largely depends, their depletion had a very bad effect on the fishery.

But the fishermen of those years had another, very expensive problem. Great numbers of whales, especially humpbacks, came close inshore trying to find their share of the scarce caplin, and in so doing got entangled in nets and fishing gear, causing untold damage and heavy financial loss.

Memorial University of Newfoundland set up a special Whale Research Unit at its St. John's campus. One of the skills the Unit has developed is that of freeing whales that are trapped in fishing gear and so saving at least a proportion of both whales and gear. A group of divers is on call, ready to go to the rescue when fishermen report trapped whales. Their success rate is impressive.

In the course of these rescues the divers seem to feel an extraordinary sense of rapport with the whales. As long as the whale remains alive and able to breathe, it seems to realize that these swimming creatures are there to help. By letting the whale see and feel them, with plenty of warning, it is possible to work at cutting away ropes and nets without causing the huge animal to panic or thrash about. A dead whale enmeshed in gear is apparently a much worse problem than a live one.

The Whale Research Unit has done a great deal to educate both fishermen and the public about whales, and to correct some of the amazing misconceptions that have existed. With modern technology revealing ever more information about them, and television letting us see whales in the wild and in captivity, they have become one of the world's most intriguing animals. When they come close to shore, as they do in Bonne Bay, it is thrilling to see them in the flesh.

Bip, the home-built dinghy which carried us to so many wonderful places.

The sound of a whale's blow, once heard, is instantly recognizable and it is this that alerts one to watch for the gliding back next time it surfaces. Living on the shore of Bonne Bay, as large and deep as it is, and surrounded by hills, one becomes aware almost at once if there is a whale in the bay. Over the years we have had some wonderful whale-watching experiences.

The same year that the pair of blue whales spent two weeks of April in Bonne Bay, a pod of humpbacks spent all summer in and out of the bay, roaming around with exuberant activity. One heard and saw them so often that they became quite commonplace. But never can a creature fifty feet long fail to thrill one when close at hand. Sailing one day near Norris Point, we saw them close by, apparently at play, or at least getting a bang (literally) out of their immense weight and strength. Repeatedly a white fore-flipper, a third of the length of the animal, would stick out of the water like a sail, then wave around and slap down. The enormous commotion they caused while swimming near the surface could have been very active fishing or just joie de vivre. It also could have been an effort to shed an irritating growth of barnacles on the skin. But whatever the cause, it led to one of them breaching — the entire whale leaping clear of the water and smashing back down with the effect a longliner might have if dropped from a davit! The power of the tail thrust that could lift this immense body out of the water was beyond imagining.

Their blows became a familiar background sound to one's work around the house and garden. But these were not the only sounds they made. When they were upwind and not too far away, we sometimes heard them singing. One calm evening they were off Mudge's Point, half a mile from the house. We paddled along in the canoe till we were quite close to them and sat silent, entranced by the sounds they were making. They stayed close together, lazily wallowing about, and we could only interpret their astonishingly varied sounds as happy social communication. The immensity of their ocean world in relation to our parochial, earth-bound milieu, together with the fact that they can communicate over vast distances with their ultra-low-frequency sounds, leaves the imagination boggling. One's mind stretches and strains trying to imagine all the news, questions, warnings or commands (and who knows, maybe jokes) that they may pass to one another. We heard their varied sounds quite often, but that calm evening they gave us a concert from another world.

We haven't seen humpbacks in Bonne Bay since that year. Sometimes months or whole seasons pass without a whale in the bay, but over the years we have become familiar with quite a few species of this magnificent mammal.

Minkes, at some twenty feet one of the smaller great whales, are usually solitary, make little sound or spray when they blow, and are inconspicuous, but we see them in all seasons. Fin whales (about sixty-five feet in length) we have seen on many occasions, usually alone. One year, however, an adult and her calf were around for a week or two.

Of the really large whales, the most unusual sighting was a sperm whale. Since they are deep ocean dwellers, it was unusual to see one in an inlet, albeit an exceptionally deep one. They are very recognizable because of their enormous size and the row of humps they have in lieu of a dorsal fin. You don't really see the shape of the strange bulbous head, but their blow is unmistakable — a rounded cloud of spray that blows forward and to the left — and unlike that of any other whale. This sperm whale's visit was brief, and we only saw him on his way back to the open sea early one summer morning.

Some of the smaller whales are impressive in their numbers and activities. Potheads (pilot whales) can suddenly appear in the bay in hundreds, though more often in smaller groups. They are extremely active and agile and, when busy fishing, give a strong impression of having fun. Some friends, out in their canoe, found themselves the object of interest of a group of pothead whales. Some of them dived shallowly under the canoe where they were seen to turn half on their sides, showing clearly the white patch on their underside, a manoeuvre they apparently perform in order to see well with the upper eye. This impression was borne out by a few who stuck their heads out of the water to look at the canoe. Here again the sense that the whales were essentially benign left the canoeists quite unafraid.

The largest school of harbour porpoise I had ever seen came charging into the bay one fall. There could have been over a thousand; the sea was alive with them, slicing through the water. The multitude drove on down the Western Arm, presumably fishing as they went. Later in the day we saw them depart, again at high speed. Coming and going, they were an impressive sight.

The most delightful acrobat of the species that we have encountered is the white-sided dolphin. In a spanking breeze we were sailing in the Western Arm one day when we saw signs of furious activity and sailed over to see what was happening. A group of dolphins parted as we sailed in among them and as we tacked about they followed us with enthusiastic leaps and acrobatics. Close to them we could see the elegant pattern on their bodies. Suddenly they had had their fun with our dinghy and took off at high speed.

Very occasionally blue-fin tuna are seen in Bonne Bay. They compare with the smaller whales in size and activity, and can be very spectacular to watch. Sleek and muscular like their small cousins the mackerel, tuna are very active in hunting other fish and their presence is invariably signalled by the wild excitement of the gulls who follow them in screaming flocks, plunging after damaged fish as the tuna attack a school. Tuna are often stimulated by the speed of fast boats and sometimes make great arching leaps out of the water. This can be quite alarming if they are close, but it is a thrilling sight nevertheless. Unfortunately the heavy and wasteful sport fishing of these splendid fish has greatly reduced their numbers. Once common in the bay, they are now seldom seen.

During the years when the seal fishery operated, one seldom saw seals in the bay. Now, in summer, an occasional group of half-grown harp seals, known as beaters, may be seen. With their shining heads bobbing, they stay in tight-knit groups, fishing and playing together.

In April, when the ice pans are drifting about on the sea and in the bay, one may catch sight of a few mothers and pups. One year we were surprised to find a little whitecoat on the beach just above the tide-wash. All by himself, he kept quite still, snarling a bit if we got too close. We thought he must be injured, or at least orphaned, and got in touch with the Park naturalist in case there was anything we should do for him.

Apparently that year there was very little ice and instead of being able to rub off their white coats on the ice many pups were coming ashore to rub themselves on the rocks. That he was alone was evidently quite normal, for their mothers abandon them as soon as they are well stocked with milk. They can swim well by then, and when they get hungry enough they start to fish for themselves. We kept an eye on this one and, sure enough, with the next high tide, having rubbed off more of his coat on the rocks, he slowly and very casually let himself be floated off by the tide. Once clear of the rocks, he was off to begin his adult life, looking very tiny but thoroughly at home in his element.

The Year's Round of Fish and Fishing

When Bonne Bay freezes over, one tends to forget all that depth of salt water beneath the ice sheet. But life seems to go on there much as usual except that, for a few weeks, the fish have a respite from the constant hunting of gulls, men and marine mammals.

For the schools of herring that have been in the bay since the fall, the intensive fishing by seiners suddenly ceases. Equipped with sonar, lights and fast speedboats that ring the schools with nets, these vessels are devastatingly efficient fishers.

The relief from hunting is broken only in mid-winter when a few fishermen use their ingenious method to catch herring through the ice. To do this, they chop a row of holes in the ice a pole's length apart and use the pole to pass the net from one hole to the next until it is fully spread. Each day the net is hauled up through one of the holes. The herring freeze almost at once on the ice and are stored, often in a deep snowbank, ready to bait the lobster pots as soon as that season opens. A few cod are also jigged through holes in the ice.

Fishing for herring through the ice.

In April the season of ice is brought to an end when the Coast Guard icebreaker comes in and with a few apparently effortless passes breaks up the ice enough for it to flow out with the tide. The lobster season, the high season of the year for the fishermen of this part of the coast, can then begin. All winter they have been building and repairing lobster-pots and these are now stacked and ready to set. The opening day of the lobster fishery is a very special one for the whole community, for it marks the end of the long winter and the start of the year's harvest of the sea. The boats set out in a rush, each piled high with pots and each man heading for his favourite berth.

Next day the families expect their traditional feast of lobster; not just a lobster each, but a glorious binge that has been looked forward to for months! But as lobsters are the mainstay of the fisherman's income, and also help provide him with the unemployment insurance benefits that he needs to see him through the winter months, few can spare as many lobsters for the family as they once could.

While the lobster season is still under way, the spring run of cod comes into the bay and can be caught with cod-jiggers — handlines with a lead weight the size and shape of a caplin, the cod's favourite food. The weight has big hooks below it and when it is jigged up and down near the bottom where the cod are feeding they get hooked when they come to investigate.

It is the schools of caplin coming in to spawn that attract the cod to the inshore waters in the spring. In early June, usually during a spell of foggy weather, the schools of caplin swarm up onto the beaches to deposit their eggs among the sand and gravel. All around the Island, the caplin scull as this is called, is an event that is eagerly watched for, and young and old alike turn out for the fun of catching their share of caplin. Many of the tasty little fish are salted or corned for future use; some are sun dried; a few are smoked; others are fresh frozen; but the bulk of the catch makes rich and effective fertilizer.

Overlapping with the end of the lobster season is the opening of the commercial salmon fishery. L-shaped nets are run out from shore to catch the salmon as they head for the rivers to spawn.

Plankton, consisting of billions of microscopic creatures, is attracted by the flow of edible matter in the tidal waters of the bay. It, in turn, attracts a great range of other predators, from herring, to squid, to the baleen whales.

The arrival of enormous schools of mackerel in August may also be associated with this rich source of food. One both sees and hears the schools of mackerel as they "boil" on the surface, their hectic activity making a sound like dry leaves blowing. And if a gull or a passing boat startles them, every fish in the school slaps its tail on the surface at once and the whole school disappears.

If they are not frightened by too much fishing, mackerel will go for red-feathered lures; they are fun to catch, as well as being good to eat. Using the small sailboat and trolling a string of six feathered lures, we've sailed slowly back and forth through a school and often got a fish on every hook at once. Chaos would ensue as we tried to get six lively and muscular mackerel aboard without losing any! When a market can be found for them, there is a commercial mackerel fishery in early fall.

Fall is the main season for fishing cod. They are abundant then on the banks off Rocky Harbour. There they are fished with baited trawl lines, jiggers, or gill-nets. If the fish are close to shore, traditional codtraps are set. A codtrap consists of a net box some fifty feet square, hung in the water, with a leader running out from the shore to a narrow gap in the net. The fish swim into the box and, unable to find their way out, are trapped.

Bonne Bay is thought to be a breeding ground for queen crab, an extraordinarily delicious crab whose long legs contain the sweet and tender meat. Because it is a breeding ground, there is no commercial fishery for them here, but a few get caught in gill-nets set near the bottom for cod.

Flounder seem to be present at all seasons but, though very good to eat, are not much in demand. Mussels, clams and scallops are all to be found as well, but not in commercial quantities.

Late in the summer the squid come in, sometimes in vast numbers. There is something about squid-jigging that generates a festive atmosphere. As soon as one boat gets "into the squid," in no time there will be half a dozen boats, all tied together, full of happy people busy jigging them. It is a messy business because of the black ink squirted by the squid, and among much laughter and teasing everyone gets filthy. It is hard to describe the taste and the texture of squid. It can be more like chewing rubber bands than anything, but the taste is unique and, if well cooked and nicely served, squid is really delicious.

As much a part of the life of the bay as the creatures that live in it are the various boats that leave their wakes upon its surface. One, whose elegant shape comes from very ancient times, is the flat-bottomed, double-ended dory. The dory is designed for rowing by two men, but rows so sweetly that a child can handle it. Stable in the water, its flat bottom allows it to be hauled out on a beach. This design also allows a number of dories to be stacked one inside the other, a great benefit to the oldtime schooners fishing off the Grand Banks. A dozen or more could be carried on deck and, upon arrival on the Banks, lowered into the water to be used by the crew to fish with handlines or trawls.

The dory is one of the simplest and most robust of utility rowing boats and is found on many of Europe's coasts. In Orkney, Shetland, France, Portugal and Spain, the design varies little except in size and decoration. From one or several of these places it must have come with the fishermen to Newfoundland. As these were all places where the Vikings ventured and held sway for a time, one cannot help wondering if they were the original designers of this useful little boat.

Being pointed at both ends, the dory will not take an outboard motor, so when these came into general use the dory design was adapted by replacing the pointed stern with a square transom. This modified dory, often referred to as a flat, is one of the most widely used inshore fishing boats. Using local lumber and "knees" cut from naturally bent spruce, most fishermen can build one in three or four days and expect it to last through as many seasons of hard use.

The sound of boats on the bay is a part of life when one lives by the shore. The heavy diesels of the Coast Guard vessels make the old house rumble whenever they enter the bay. Some of the local longliners have their own distinctive engine sounds, and one gets to know who is passing without looking up. With the first light of dawn on summer mornings the busy outboards buzz by on their way to the lobster pots or the salmon nets.

But the one sound above all others that arouses one's nostalgia for the Newfoundland fishery of years gone by is that of the old trap boats with a "make-and-break" engine, a few of which are still in use around the bay. They are the simplest, toughest and most reliable of motors. With a single cylinder and a heavy fly-wheel, one engine might serve a succession of boats, and probably a couple of generations of fishermen. The sharp, rapid, crack! crack! crack! as one of these old inboard engines passes by echoes around the bay and recalls a time when they were the universal power of the Newfoundland fishing fleet.

CHAPTER 6

Through The Gulch

The Land from Below the Ocean

If there is one feature that convinced the powers that be that the Bonne Bay area should be recognized and protected as a national park, it was most likely the Tableland, a very special piece of geography between the Western Arm of Bonne Bay and the coast. The Tableland is one of the world's outstanding and most visible demonstrations of the forces that have shaped the continents of the world as we know them. It is also one of the best exposures of the material of the earth's mantle which normally lies many miles below the crust on which we live. The rocks under your feet there are the very same material as that which lines the floors of the deepest oceans.

Such up-thrusts of ocean floor, or earth mantle, are rare but not unique. Western Newfoundland has several examples, one of which you can see from the Trans Canada Highway above Corner Brook. The bare plateau of the Blomidon Mountains fills a huge area just south of the Bay of Islands and looks very like the Tableland. There are a number of other outcrops widely scattered across the world.

The Tableland's very special geology, and the plantlife related to it, draw geologists and botanists from all over the world. The knowledgeable amateur in these fields, and even the most casual observer, can find a wealth of interest in this remarkable terrain. Across its top there is a line, discernable at least to geologists, which shows where mantle ends and crust begins. The west end, they tell us, was nearest the surface, and the end near Bonne Bay was deep within the earth before the forces that shifted the continents broke loose a huge fragment of mantle and forced it up to overlap the crust and form this 2000-foot mountain.

The rock itself is like no rock you normally see. Broken pieces reveal that it is really black. The golden colour is caused by the magnesium and iron that it contains, oxidizing and weathering in the air. Interspersed with the rock, known as peridotite, are layers of serpentine — a green, blue, black or sometimes pink substance which can look like a beautiful pottery glaze — covering the surface of many rocks you see in the Gulch. So prolific is it that the mountain is often referred to as the Serpentine Tableland.

Because this mountain does not belong on the surface, its whole chemistry is unusual and many of the plants that grow readily all around cannot grow on it. Some of those that can and do are rare and of special interest to botanists.

The Tableland has another asset that makes it a major feature of the National Park: it stands right beside a highway, Route 431. From Woody Point, this road climbs dramatically to nearly nine hundred feet and is perhaps the most scenic road in all this scenic province. It drops down a little to run through the famous Trout River Gulch, the extraordinary valley with the golden Tableland on one side and Halfway Cliff and green rolling hills on the other.

Driving through the Gulch one gets an impressive view of the landscape which looks more like part of Nevada than anything you would expect to see in Newfoundland. But to appreciate the unusual nature of its rocks and plants, you need to explore on foot. Where the old and the new roads meet there is a parking lot, and nearby the Park has an excellent interpretive exhibit concerning the Tableland. If you walk along the old road leading into the canyon of Winterhouse Brook, you realize that the landscape is not by any means as bare as it seems; it is, in fact, a natural rock garden, rich in plants, many of which you may never have seen before. Because there is none of the usual groundcover or forest, the plants that do grow are unprotected among the rocks and have to cope with a sub-arctic climate. The winter here is harsh, with tearing winds, a lot of snow, and temperatures as low as -30°C.

Early in summer, lapland rosebay (*Rhododendron lapponicum*) is in flower. It is a true rhododendron only six to twelve inches high with tiny, brilliant cerise flowers. Isolated plants often grow in the most inhospitable places, even among steeply tumbled rocks, but in some areas on the plateau it grows in large clumps. Another early gem is the yellow moccasin orchid which grows where the gabbro, or crust material, meets the serpentine. Rather surprisingly, some of the finest specimens of pitcher plants can be found among the rocks where streams run off the mountain. There are also great masses of them in the bogs beside the road, but there their beautiful pitcher leaves are buried among the grasses and only their dark bronze heads stand out. Thrift is a charming relative of the carnation and thrives here, its round pink heads held six inches high on stiff stems with all the needle-like leaves at the bottom. I associate thrift with the seaside grassy links of Scotland and have seen it nowhere else in North America. (I have not even been able to find it in any of my three North American flower books.) Some of the most plentiful flowers in the Gulch are the blue hare bells — a joy to behold blowing in the wind. Yellow stonecrop and tiny cinquefoils are everywhere, but perhaps my favourite is the moss campion whose smooth green mounds are fitted neatly among the rocks and covered with minute pink stars. One plant that I treasure for its name alone is almost too tiny to see: the lesser pussytoes. A botanical friend identified one for me. It was growing all alone in the gravel of a wind-scoured mound known as the Pimple.

The flowers we see in the Gulch in summer show little sign of the harsh winters they endure, but not so the trees and shrubs (for some do survive there). Arctic willow is beaten flat to the ground, but flowers profusely, producing fluffy seeds that bowl along in the wind. The ground juniper straggles outwards with twisted and convoluted stems, yards away from its root, and often with only a strand of life in a dry and silvered stem. Larches or tamaracks are beaten into twisted and crippled shapes in this merciless environment, eventually becoming wonderfully shaped silver skeletons standing year after year. Potentilla seems to be one of the toughest survivors; the shrub will grow to two or three feet in height and produce a mass of cheerful yellow flowers. It looks as unaffected by the harsh climate as it might growing in one's garden.

Being so close to the road, the Tableland is the most accessible mountain in Newfoundland. Its summit is only 350 feet lower than Gros Morne, but from your car you can be on the 2000 foot rim of the plateau in an hour. The easiest route lies a little to the east of the parking lot where a stream falls from the lip of a big eroded bowl in the side of the mountain. This bowl is filled with snow in winter and often has a patch that lasts all summer. Branching either left or right around the lip of the bowl, the climb to the plateau's edge is no more than a steep scramble. To walk all around the rim of the Winterhouse Brook Canyon takes about four hours, but it is one of the most thrilling hikes in the Park, with rocks, flowers and views all quite beyond the ordinary. Reaching the top of the escarpment and looking across the expanse of rock-strewn plateau before you, you may wonder if you have stepped out onto the surface of the moon.

It is a long rocky walk, about four miles, across the level top of the Tableland to reach the southern escarpment. But the view from there, down onto the Trout River Ponds and across to the totally different hills of the Gregory Plateau, is worth the effort. Rock ptarmigan are often found on the Tableland and their throaty cackle of alarm is usually the first you know of their presence.

Although the Tableland is close to the road, it is no small mountain and should be treated with respect. The plateau is flat and featureless and no place to get socked in by cloud. No one should attempt it in poor weather, or without all the normal requisites of a mountain expedition — good boots, map, compass, food and spare clothes, and a sharp eye for a change in the weather. There are only certain places where you can safely climb it, and if in doubt it is best to come down the way you went up.

On the rim of the great eroded canyon of Winterhouse Brook.

Nights on a Bald Mountain

So much of our experience of the world of nature takes place in daylight that we sometimes forget that it is all still there, still full of activity and beauty and sometimes menace, while we sleep the nights away. Just occasionally the experience of night in the open tells us how much we miss.

A friend spent the summer doing geological field work on the Tableland. She camped up there most of the time, enjoying the nights of space and solitude...until one night when a sudden summer thunderstorm enveloped her and she found herself completely at the mercy of the elements. Unable to do anything to protect herself, she just had to accept whatever might happen. On that bare rock-field the continuous flashes of lightning and deafening roar of thunder rent the darkness with devastating power and violence, the wind driving the rain in solid gusts of water. Eventually the tempest passed and the thunder rolled away into the distance. Shaken and soaked, she was left unharmed. But for the rest of her life, when the thunder rolls, she will remember the storm that night on the Tableland.

The Northern Lights, too, once seen in extraordinary circumstances up there, trigger the memory whenever I see them.

One sparkling day in March, two friends and I climbed the Tableland. Cocoa the poodle, who enjoyed such winter outings as much as we did, was with us. A few days before there had been a thaw and heavy rain, but this day was clear and still and very cold. The mountain shone with frozen snow-crust and its breathtaking beauty should have given us fair warning, but as we climbed up by one of the gullies inside the big canyon, the snow there was soft and gave us good footing. Exhilarated with the sun and the beauty all around us, we walked over the top to look down onto the Trout River Ponds and across to the Gregory Plateau beyond. The going was the best we had ever found there and we travelled quickly over the hard crust.

We decided to come down by a different route that would bring us closer to our car, but soon discovered that on the north slope the ice was so hard that we could not kick steps in it. Not wanting to risk a slip down such a dangerous slope, we tried another gully a few miles to the west but that was just as treacherous. We were still looking for a way to get down when the setting sun turned the snow-covered mountain to sugar-pink and we realized that the only thing to do was to use the remaining daylight to go all the way back to the gully we had climbed that morning.

Our steps dragged. Cocoa was tired and let us know he had had enough of our wanderings and wanted his supper. Darkness fell as we trudged along, but he unerringly led us to the spot where our footsteps emerged from the canyon. He was all for going right on down — easy enough for him, but impossible for us in the dark. Knowing that the moon (which was close to full and would give us enough light to see our way down) would rise in a few hours, we sat down to wait, huddled together to keep warm, with an impatient poodle in our midst.

Very gradually a glow developed in the northern sky and soon we saw a few dim shafts of the Northern Lights. By eerie leaps and shimmers and bursts of light the Aurora grew, first white, then ghostly green, and then a glow of red that disappeared when you looked at it and came again as you looked away. It gradually lit up the whole northern sky in a display such as one seldom sees. We were so entranced watching it that it was some time before we realized it was light enough to pick our way down the gully. Cocoa in the lead, we set off, hoping the heavenly display would last till we got down — and so it did, dying away as we reached the bottom of the canyon.

Reflections in the cove, Curzon Village.

Winter light in Curzon Village. Across the cove stands the lighthouse at Woody Point.

Snug amid deep snow, the old house looks across to Norris Point and Gros Morne.

A gale sends gusts of spray scudding across the bay.

A black swallowtail visits the garden.

A midsummer sunrise behind Gros Morne.

"Bonne Bay sky" — the astonishing 'sculptured' clouds that occasionally form over Bonne Bay.

59

Gulls and shining water in the late fall herring season.

On the opening day of the lobster season, the boats set out loaded to the gunwales.

The golden Tableland, dotted with snow, contrasts with the green hills of the Western Arm.

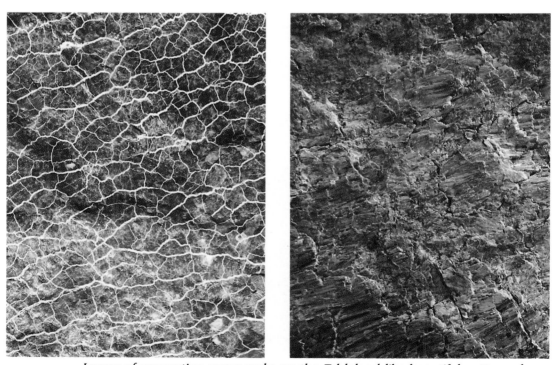

Layers of serpentine cover rocks on the Tableland like beautiful pottery glazes.

Thrift (left) and harebells (right) thrive in the harsh environment of the Gulch.

Distant view of Trout River.

62

The river-mouth at Trout River, centre of the town's busy summer fishery.

Gisela Westphalen

A fine view of the narrows of the Trout River Ponds, my reward for a steep scamble up Elephant Head.

Morning mist over Rocky Harbour Pond, tranquilly reflecting Gros Morne.

Crow Cliff in winter can look as imposing as its larger neighbour, Gros Morne.

Gisela Westphalen

Energy flowed back with relief as we strode along in the starlight to our waiting car. Although we had not been in any real danger, as experienced hikers long familiar with the Tableland in all its moods we felt ashamed at our misjudgement.

The day on the mountain was one to remember, but coming down by the light of the Aurora was a magical experience. I can never see the Northern Lights without reliving that night on the bare mountain.

Trout River

The fishing community of Trout River, just outside the southwest corner of the Park, is unique even among Newfoundland's wealth of distinctive coastal communities. The twelve-mile road linking Trout River to Woody Point was a mere cart-track until the middle 1950s when the first rough road was built. Isolated for so many years, and cut off for much of every winter by storms and snowdrifts in the Gulch even after the road went through, the Trout River people are staunchly individualistic. Both they and their community have a character all their own.

There was a time, when the first plans for the new park were being drawn up, when it was suggested that the lovely cove, river and hills of Trout River should all be restored to their natural state as a major feature of the Park. This would have involved relocating the nine hundred inhabitants and erasing all trace of their habitation. Faced with this daunting proposal, the determined independence of the people was such that, by sheer passive resistance, they forestalled any attempt by Parks Canada to put this plan into effect. Without recourse to demonstrations or concerted action of any kind, they let it be known that they would not give up their birthright on any account. The planners relocated the proposed boundary instead!

Fishing is the main industry of the settlement. Most of the fishermen's sheds, the community wharves, and the big warehouses for saltfish are concentrated on the point where the river runs out. All the larger fishing boats tie up there and men are busy unloading and cleaning fish all through the fishing season. At the corner of the road the older fishermen congregate to watch the comings and goings, pass away the time, and have a "cuffer" about the catch and the price of fish. The spot is known as Cuffer Corner.

The first man to settle in Trout River was a George Crocker, and Crockers still form the longest list of names in the Trout River telephone directory. It was a natural place to settle. The bay, though exposed to the prevailing westerly winds, has high cliffs to the north and the south which give it some protection. The sandy beach provides a safe landing for the flat-bottomed dories, and the deep mouth of the river gives shelter for larger boats. Caplin swarm onto the beaches every June and in earlier years the river had a good run of salmon and trout. Inland, two long ponds give access in summer and winter to the interior for both logging and hunting. Above all, there is abundant level, arable land. Over the years the settlers cleared the nearby woods to create pasture for large numbers of sheep, cattle and horses.

As the settlement developed, agriculture became a small industry, second to fishing. In spite of losing to the Park the large grazing areas at Green Gardens and Lomond, Trout River people still raise a lot of animals and grow some of the best potatoes to be had. To compensate for the lost grazing areas, the Park and the Department of Agriculture are helping the Trout River farmers to make a large community pasture just beyond the new campground. The area lies in a wide valley where belts of trees are interspersed with extensive natural meadows that were once bogland. Oddly enough, long before the national park came on the scene, this fertile valley was always referred to by Trout River people as The Park.

The high land to the south of this valley extends to the shore of Bay of Islands and is known as the Gregory Plateau. It is the home territory of the Gregory caribou herd. On the coast, some twelve miles south of Trout River, is the beautiful but deserted settlement of Chimney Cove. This whole area, with its fine coastal and wilderness scenery and its caribou, was originally recommended for inclusion in the national park. It is unfortunate that it had to be left out.

There is an interesting geographical aspect to the arable land of Trout River: it is on two levels. Alongside the river is the usual rich silt of a river valley. About a hundred feet above this is a large level area where, aeons ago, the sea level used to be. It is now a raised beach with surf-rounded pebbles and ancient seashells embedded in it. A good layer of soil has formed on top, due partly to the practice of enriching the soil with caplin. Many homes have been built up on this level, but the majority are located around the cove and along the river bank.

On the south side of the river, below the bridge, the community has created a pleasant picnic site and lookout trail, close to a high rock pinnacle known as The Old Man. From there, it is also possible to make one's way out to the lighthouse on the south point of the bay. This is a spectacular spot from which to look out over the town and the bustling activity around the river-mouth.

Southward from the lighthouse there is about a mile of easy walking along green cliff tops very similar to those at Green Gardens. This section of coast is exceptionally wild and rugged. The jagged cliffs, sea stacks, reefs and islets are impressive at any time, but in a gale the inshore water becomes a swirling tumult of white and green as the waves crash and burst, filling the air with spray. Nothing can be heard above the roar of wind and water.

On a tranquil evening, however, those cliff tops are a lovely place on which to sit and watch the sun set over the Gulf. At any time of day there is always something to see: boats coming and going; fishermen hauling their gear; and always, the ceaseless wheeling and crying of the gulls.

Close to the Trout River Ponds is a particularly well-located Park campsite. Sheltered by trees, it still has marvelous views up the Trout River Ponds and is an ideal base from which to explore the whole southwest corner of the Park.

The Trout River Ponds and the Overfall

The two Trout River Ponds run twelve miles inland from the river outlet just above the community. Where the two are separated by a gravel bar, a domed hill stands some 1300 feet high on the south side. Its old name is Narrows Head, but its shape strongly suggests an elephant's head and so it is often referred to as Elephant Head. As you approach it, travelling down the four miles of the outer pond, the features become quite distinct. Below the rounded crest, two black cliffs suggest deep eye sockets and ears; between them a grey rocky ridge looks like a wrinkled trunk, curving down to drink at the pond. From the top you can see all around — to the community, the ponds, and the Tableland, and southward to the Gregory Plateau. The hilltop is carpeted with such alpine plants as diapensia, whose creamy blossoms thrive in the constant breeze.

Linking the two ponds is a fast-flowing narrows which cuts through the gravel bank. It is a curious place, for, on the Tableland side, the pebbles forming the bank are all rusty gold, while only twenty feet across the water those on the other bank are grey.

Once you pass the narrows the extraordinary inner pond is revealed. It can rival any other feature in the Park — including Western Brook Pond — for, although only a mile across, its two sides are totally different landscapes. On the north shore the Tableland drops steeply to the water, all bare golden rock, while steep, bright green bluffs and grey cliffs line the whole length of the south side. On a fine, calm summer day the multicoloured surroundings and their reflections in the water seem almost unreal. A boat trip in there is indeed a unique experience.

The Park's southern boundary lies close to the Trout River Ponds but has an extension that includes a little bit of the Gregory Plateau and a very lovely waterfall which drops from the rim of the plateau to join the upper Trout River. Called the Overfall, it is one of the gems of the Park but is, unfortunately, just out of sight from the end of the pond and very hard to reach except by helicopter.

On my second visit to the Overfall, I saw its full height from the helicopter.

We had had distant, tantalizing glimpses of the Overfall from the top of Pic à Tenerife, from the plateau above Mackenzie's Brook and from the south rim of the Tableland. It looks inaccessible on the map and we could see no way to get to it. We were not really aiming for it the day we took the little sailboat, Bip, over to Trout River Pond with gear and food for two days' camping. We thought of sailing in to the end of the inner Trout River Pond and camping there, maybe catching a few trout in the brooks that run into it.

Down the length of the outer pond we had a fine sail with a strong westerly wind behind us. With a neatly judged dash against the current we were through the narrows and into the inner pond. The steep escarpment of the Tableland was now lit up in glorious gold by the afternoon sun and patches of late snow glinted in the high crevices. The wind had died and the whole rampart was reflected in the still water, a marvelous blend of blue and gold and bronze.

Across the pond, the bluffs became grey cliffs, dropping sheer into the water. Above them were jagged pinnacles among the green, and a rocky skyline. These gave way to a steep scree slope that ran down from a rounded ridge to a small point. The slope of tumbled rocks looked climbable and the point seemed to be a suitable place to camp. Our topographical map showed that, once on the top, we should be able to reach the Overfall by hiking along the edge of the plateau.

It was worth a try and we set up camp.

Early next morning we were off, with Cocoa, our hardy and much-travelled brown poodle, in the lead. The scree slope presented no problem, but the top was very hard going with frequent dips and hollows, each filled with a tangle of wind-flattened spruce known as tuckamore, or tuck. Ridges, small ponds and bands of tuck made for a slow zig-zag route. For easier walking we made good use of every snow patch that lay in our path. It was late afternoon before we finally reached the Overfall.

What a spot it is! The stream runs for only a few yards out of a large pond before it leaps over the edge of a precipice. An overhanging rock right alongside provides a good, if frightening viewpoint from which one can look straight down the fall. Far below the water smashes onto fallen rocks, raising a great cloud of spray before the stream disappears into the forest to join the Upper Trout River.

Although we found a slightly better route back to our camp, it still took us five hours of the toughest travelling we had ever done, and that added up to an arduous eleven hour hike. Cocoa, his feet sore from the tuck, ate his supper lying down in the tent. He demanded, and received, full sick-privileges that night and made a nest for himself on the ends of our sleeping bags.

The inner pond was as calm as a mill pond next morning, and we rowed for several miles, watching the gently wavering reflections. Once clear of the sheltered inner pond, the westerly wind blew against us and it took a long series of tacks to bring us back to the car.

As so often, there were men and boys with their boats by the shore of the pond and they watched us sail in with some interest. The skills their grandfathers had in sailing boats have long been lost in the welter of hard-working outboard motors, and most fishermen are somewhat distrustful of pleasure-craft and the people who use them. But as they had often seen us sailing there before, we seemed to pass muster as sailors of a sort and they gladly lent a hand to carry Bip up onto the trailer for the short drive home.

When the outer Trout River Pond is frozen and the logging season underway, it becomes a highway for innumerable men, horses and snowmobiles. The timber supplies lie mostly toward Chimney Cove Brook, and it is nothing to see a dozen or more slides loaded with logs, heading back to the town. This is obviously an activity the men enjoy, for there is much banter and laughter and a festive mood prevails. Even the hard-working ponies seem to enjoy their work, their main function of the year.

All this activity on the pond makes it a delightful place for an outing on cross-country skis. With a few inches of snow on the ice, as there usually are, it is a fine ski run in to the gravel bar that divides the two ponds. The inner pond is so immensely deep, however, that it seldom has safe, bearing ice, even in March, and unless there were fresh snowmobile tracks I would not venture out onto it.

One day in late winter we sat on a fallen log to have lunch and enjoy the view of the inner pond. Although the temperature was very low, the ice there was thin and had a pattern of crack lines running in all directions. There had recently been a spring thaw and a lot of water was running out of the ponds, causing a sudden change in the water level. There was the most astonishing concert of eerie sounds from that straining ice sheet — long deep booms, pings, hissing and whistling sounds, all at varying pitches and intervals. The effect was of the most wonderful "space" music. We sat entranced for an hour or more until the chill drove us onto our feet and skis again for the hour's run back to Trout River.

Winter evening darkened the sky and in the village the last ponies and slides were heading home. The still cold air was full of many scents — of ponies, and of resin from the newly-cut logs they pulled; of wood smoke that curled from every chimney; of food cooking in busy kitchens; and somewhere, underlying all the other scents, the ever-present whiff of fish.

Green Gardens

Green Gardens, a three-mile section of the coast lying between Trout River and the mouth of Bonne Bay, is a long, lush green meadow on the cliff tops, bordered above by a steep ridge of forest. Until the area became part of the Park it was literally a place of green gardens where the people of Trout River grew hay, potatoes and vegetables in tightly-fenced plots while their animals grazed the surrounding grassland. Every spring the animals would be driven over the hills from Trout River or carried round by boat. The sheep and horses still know the way there and, despite the efforts of their owners to prevent them, they will head for Green Gardens whenever they get the chance!

It is a splendid section of coast with high and varied cliffs. Most of them are volcanic in origin, some red, some black seamed with white, some with superb examples of pillow lava formed in an undersea eruption caused by the shifting continents. There are several sea stacks, and a fine cave as well. The beaches are piled high with driftwood and the bric-a-brac of the sea, for both wind and tide tend to set toward this shore.

In the cliffs themselves are many maritime plants that grow only where the sea wind blows. Watching the sea from those cliffs, you might sight a whale. The most likely would be a solitary minke whale, or a group of potheads (pilot whales) whose big, bulbous heads make them easy to recognize. Porpoises and dolphins are also fairly common. A more unusual sighting would be one of the great whales, a humpback or a fin whale, whose huge blow is usually the first indication of their presence.

Near the south end of Green Gardens, and accessible only at low tide, is an unusual sea cave. From the foot of the steps that lead down to the beach from the campsite, it is just around the second point going northward. It is not a deep cave, but wide and rather symmetrical, and always reminds me of a theatre stage. At the back is a smooth wall of rock; at the sides curtains of eroded and layered rock that form the wings of the stage; and at the front a symmetrical proscenium arch. Here the resemblance ends, for the cave is floored with large boulders, rounded by the waves. One should not linger too long here; it is not a cosy place in which to wait out the hours till the next low tide!

The Green Gardens trail is one of the most varied in the Park. It starts out over a rugged expanse of Tableland rock and crosses a bare ridge where there is a junction and a choice of trails. The more southerly trail is shorter and leads down through an open valley and along wooded slopes to the south end of the cliffs. The longer one strikes northward and reaches the north end by way of Wallace's Brook. Both trails have many steps as they drop down to sea level from a height of 750 feet in the Gulch.

The round trip of these trails is a long and strenuous one if done in one day, but it is an outstanding backpacking trip if you camp overnight on the cliff tops. A very satisfactory day's outing is to go and return by the trail to the south end of the Gardens, spending a few hours exploring the cliffs and beaches and having a boil-up on one of the campsite fireplaces.

Soon after the Green Gardens trail was built we made the round of it and camped overnight at the northern of the two bivouac campsites. We were woken in the night by the curious and eerie cough-screech of a fox barking. He was evidently intrigued and a bit scared by our tent and made a complete circle, barking at intervals. Our dog was thoroughly spooked by the sound and crept inside for safety. Unfortunately it was too dark to be able to see the fox. We had just settled down after this excitement when we felt the ground shake with heavy, rapid thuds. This time it was horses, probably also spooked by the fox, galloping past in the night. Luckily our tent had no guy-ropes or it might have gone with them!

But our first visit to Green Gardens was in winter, some years before the Park built the trail. It was no easy place to get to then, except by the old sheep path from Trout River, but we decided to try going via Wallace's Brook and were depending on enough snowcover remaining on that April day for us to be able to travel on snowshoes.

Wallace's Brook runs down the Gulch, and where the road swings southwest to Trout River the brook makes off to the northwest to meet the sea, some four miles away. The ice on the brook was already starting to break up but, keeping to the sides, we made it safely to the mouth. The Gulf of St. Lawrence was still solid with ice, tight to the shore, so we made our way on the sea ice to the low cliffs at the north end of Green Gardens.

That day the meadowland on the top of the cliffs was a sheet of very slippery wet ice, reflecting all the colours of the sky. After the long miles on heavy snow, and then on slippery ice, we hoped to find the old sheep path at the south end and so have an easy walk over to Trout River. We failed to locate it in the snow, however, and had much rough going through the woods before we emerged on the bare hilltops at the north end of Trout River.

It was a good day's hike, but the memory of it certainly makes me appreciate the easy walking on today's well-constructed trails!

The volcanic cliffs and rugged shore at Green Gardens are splendid at any time of year.

CHAPTER 7

The North Shore of Bonne Bay

Gros Morne

Like many names on this coast, the name Gros Morne originates from the years of French occupation, but the present-day pronunciation has been anglicised so that the 's' of *Gros* is pronounced. As the French word *Morne* suggests gloomy or brooding, it seems that whoever named it *Big Gloomy* was perhaps only there in the cold, grey, sunless months of early winter, for then the name aptly describes the mountain. Once it is glistening white with snow, however, it is anything but gloomy. Standing out as it does from the main range, Gros Morne often catches a searchlight of winter sun and glows almost as though it were lit from within. On a summer's day its pale grey rock looks almost pink in the bright sun, and with its pattern of corries on the south side and green terraces on the north, it is a most handsome mountain.

The trail to the top of Gros Morne starts close to sea level at the head of Deer Arm. One of the longest and best hikes in the Park, it loops over the top of the mountain and comes down by way of the side valley, known as the Ferry Gulch, giving a wide variety of terrain and views that span most of the Park. The trail is named after James Callahan, Prime Minister of Great Britain in the late 1970s and a staunch protector of the world's green places.

For the first thousand feet the trail climbs through thick woods abounding with plants. Of the many animals that live there squirrels, a recent import to the island, are the boldest and most likely to be seen. They are usually heard too — protesting one's presence with a flow of invective from a branch overhead! Weasels and snowshoe hares are common but they avoid people, as do the foxes, and the mink and otter which frequent the streams.

Nearing the open valley of the Ferry Gulch, the trail cuts through sections of tuck (tuckamore, or krummholz), that mat of small spruce or fir that is beaten down by the snow and the wind till it is about as penetrable as shrunk knitting. Try moving off the track a few steps and you realize that Park trails give a deceptive impression of the realities of moving around in Newfoundland's wilderness terrain! Before the advent of the Park, almost the only way to approach Gros Morne was to follow the watercourse up into this same valley.

The little ponds and streams that you find in the valley at the foot of the scree slope of the mountain are often used by beavers. And before there were so many people around, we also found green-winged teal nesting there.

Beyond the valley, the climb becomes a steep scramble up the V of a rocky gully. As it faces due south it can be a very hot climb, but there are ample rewards for your efforts for already the views over Bonne Bay are stunning. As you go higher, your eye sweeps over mile upon rolling mile of the high tops of the Long Range.

One of the most likely places to catch sight of that rare, huge and handsome rabbit, the arctic hare, is just as you come out of the steep gully and are surrounded by more gently sloping scree. Stand still a minute and scan all around; arctic hares are fantastically well camouflaged among these rocks and they take full advantage of this by sitting still, even as you get quite close. Early in summer their last tufts of white winter coat among the new grey fur match the pebbles of white quartz and the little snow patches; in their full summer coat their backs are a beautiful rich grey and their extra-long ears as black as pitch. They must weigh as much as a beagle! It is small wonder they were popular as a source of meat and hence were heavily over-hunted. As they are a true arctic animal, the Park is about the southern limit of their range. Appropriately, they are the symbol of Gros Morne National Park.

The snowshoe hare of the lower, wooded areas has a very different coat. A rather untidy brownish colour, it is splotched with white in the spring. They too are well camouflaged in their own environment.

The plateau of Gros Morne is a likely place to find rock ptarmigan, also very difficult to see among the rocks in their grey and white spring plumage; the plain grey of summer is no easier. Their growing broods of young stay chummily together and they obey their mother if she gives the order to keep still. It once took me twenty minutes to pick out a dozen chicks that were all around me in a small rock gully.

The Park trail on the top is clearly marked, but as the going up there is naturally fairly smooth not much trail-building was required. If the clouds come down it is wise to keep careful track of the markers as it is a bad place to get lost.

The trail takes you across to the north side of the mountain which is very steep and drops in two big terraces to Ten Mile Pond. In this magnificent valley, you can see how, thousands of years ago, the glaciers scraped and ground their way seaward leaving this sweeping U-shaped curve.

At the east end of the mountain the trail drops down to the pass at the top of the Ferry Gulch where there is a small pond and campsite for backpackers. On a recent hike there, we watched a fine bull moose who found himself on the trail between two lots of approaching hikers. To avoid them, he took off up the side of the mountain and was last seen splendidly outlined against the sky. It was there too that we were lucky enough to see a very rare gyrfalcon, cruising magnificently along the mountainside, its pale plumage sharply contrasted against the green.

Descending fairly gradually, and in places cleverly built into the side of the scree slopes, the trail completes the loop and rejoins the main trail near the small ponds at the lower end of the valley.

The round of the James Callahan trail takes about six hours. As it is wilderness country and the rock gully is hard going, boots are a must. So too is a day-pack with spare clothes, fly-dope and food. Both weather and temperature can change with little warning.

A winter climb up Gros Morne calls for snowshoes. The Park trail will be buried deep under snow and the climb through the woods is heavy going.

Moose like to make use of the trails that man has provided and their piston-like legs drive deep holes in the snow. Lesser creatures will have crossed the path too and

Ten Mile Pond valley with the terraced north side of Gros Morne and the blue Gulf beyond — one of the loveliest spots I have found anywhere in the Park.

are fun to identify by their footprints. Weasels, and their larger cousins, the mink, move in bounds, their pairs of prints well spaced out. A squirrel's trail can look similar, but one usually sees where he has climbed a tree. Snowshoe hares make what look like three-legged tracks that come in all sizes since there are young ones about at almost any time of year. The fat, short-tailed vole cuts quite a swath in the soft snow as though he swims through it, and is quite comic to watch if you chance to see him. The most charming of all the tracks are those of the fingertip-sized shrews whose perfect hand and foot prints are almost unbelievably tiny. A neat straight line of holes will be fox prints, for their back feet follow in the same track as the front ones.

When you come out of the woods into the valley you are likely to see where willow ptarmigan have plummeted down into the soft snow to reach the feed in the low scrub below. On cold winter nights they will roost there, comfortably sheltered from the wind. Their well-feathered legs leave characteristic prints as they search for food, and a perfect imprint of wings and tail shows where they have taken off again. But woe betide them if, as they roost, drifting snow is followed by a swift thaw and freeze for then they can be trapped under the crust. A friend once rescued dozens of them from such imprisonment.

On one memorable winter climb, just at the top of the gully, we came upon two splendid foxes — a big black and silver male and his dark red mate. Surprisingly unafraid, they sat for a long time sizing us up before quietly moving off together toward the west end of the mountain. The pelt of the male must have been worth hundreds of dollars and it was good to know that trapping had ceased within the Park and that he would go on to breed more splendid animals like himself.

On a brilliant day in March the top of Gros Morne is a wonderful place to be. The rocks are all covered with snow and one travels fast on the hard crust. Later in the winter conditions can be tricky with an icy crust or melting snow. As we were coming down through the woods late in the winter one year, the snow had softened with the day's sun causing the sudden and comic disappearance of the leader of our party. Walking across an open patch of snow, she suddenly found herself six feet down and standing among a forest of small trees, the snow crust above her head. Helpless with laughter, and with no firm footing anywhere around, she took a long time to struggle out!

Close to Gros Morne, and starting from the same parking lot, is a fine cross-country ski route. An old woods trail leads into the beautiful curving valley on the south side of Crow Cliff, Gros Morne's smaller neighbour. When the river there is well frozen and there is plenty of snow, one can follow the valley right up to the cascades and falls where the river drops from a small pond. To reach the falls and return takes about six hours — a good day's outing, especially with a boil-up in some sheltered spot near the falls.

Another good ski-run is to Ten Mile Pond, below the north flank of Gros Morne. It is also a popular snowmobile route, so one can usually follow the tracks of these machines right to the pond. Almost inaccessible in summer, this superb pond and valley are a magnificent trip in the winter months.

Rocky Harbour

In the last century, when people came to the west coast of Newfoundland from other parts of the island or from the West of England, Rocky Harbour was a natural place for them to settle. There was good fishing just offshore; the rocky coast was a good lobstering ground; and the sheltered harbour at the mouth of Bonne Bay gave ready access to the markets there for the dried cod, salt herring and canned lobster that they produced. The level land around the harbour made possible the subsistence farming and gardening so necessary to their success as settlers. Rocky Harbour soon became one of the major fishing harbours of the northwest coast.

Some experienced boat-builders were among the early settlers. With good timber stands nearby and a shelving shore in the harbour that provided a natural haul-out and launching place, they began to build fishing vessels. One that they designed came to be known as a Rocky Harbour Skiff. With two masts and three sails, it weighed some fifteen tons and gained a good reputation as a tough and reliable fishing vessel. Much later, in the fishery boom of the 1960s, a vessel called a Longliner came into being. The design proved very successful, and soon every serious fisherman strove to obtain one. Boat-building in Rocky Harbour expanded to meet the need, and both Shears' and Pittman's yards built these sturdy and handsome vessels.

When, in the late 1960s, it was proposed to make the whole area from Trout River to Parsons Pond a new national park it became apparent that, as Rocky Harbour was in the geographical centre of the area, it would most likely become the location of the new park's headquarters and main facilities. For a small fishing town on a remote coast, the changes would be considerable and people were of many minds about the prospects. Some were just apprehensive at the thought of all the visitors who would come; others could see only the inevitable restrictions on hunting and logging (and indeed for those who had always relied on these resources for part of their subsistence the outlook was bleak); and for many the influx of strangers who would come to live in the town posed something of a threat to the old and settled ways of living. But others, with an eye to economic improvements, saw business opportunities, new kinds of jobs that would keep local people employed in their own area, and improvements to schools, medical and municipal services. And so the coming of Gros Morne National Park met with a mixed reception in this, as in all the other enclave communities of the area.

With the establishment of the Park at the beginning of the 1970s, these prospects became reality. Building work of all kinds brought a welcome rush of jobs: roads, trails, houses, offices and visitor facilities had to be built, and for those people who were moving out of the smaller settlements, new homes had to be provided in the enclave communities. The building program has been continuous since that time and the Rocky Harbour of today, with streets and subdivisions of fine new houses, has grown and developed almost beyond recognition. In contrast to many national parks where staff quarters are all grouped together, here they are scattered throughout the community so that new comers and livyers get to know each other as neighbours.

The Park Headquarters, a complex of modest proportions, is sheltered in a wooded area very close to the community. The Visitors' Centre, on the other hand, is quite conspicuous. Located about four miles out in the country toward Gros Morne, it is an unconventional building, strongly suggesting a ship sailing in an ocean of trees. Inside, the building is interestingly designed and highly functional.

Over the main information desk is a large and handsome wall-hanging, a map of Bonne Bay in beautiful ranges of colours showing the various ecological regions of the area. It is done in the traditional hooking technique for which the women of this coast and of the Labrador are famous. Commissioned in 1978, the hanging was hooked in the Woody Point studio of the Bonne Bay Weavers by six ladies from Shoal Brook, Woody Point and Curzon Village. The problem of working on so large a piece of hooking was solved when the biggest quilting frame in the district was found in an attic and adapted for hooking. Once the materials had arrived — burlap from the jute mills of Scotland and wools from Denmark — the six ladies set to work. Happy to be depicting their beloved Bonne Bay on this impressive piece, the hooks fairly flew and the whole eight by six foot tapestry was completed in four weeks.

The hooks fly as work begins on the big hooked tapestry that now hangs in the Park Visitors' Centre.

Hooking mats to cover the scrubbed wooden floors of the home was one of the main winter jobs for the housewife of yesteryear. It is sad that, with the modernization of houses, hooked mats simply no longer fit in so that, in just one generation, this wonderful skill is being lost. One is all the more delighted that this wall-hanging is being seen and enjoyed by so many people and that it commemorates this old and very skilled Newfoundland craft.

The lighthouse on Lobster Cove Head, marking the entrance to Rocky Harbour and also to Bonne Bay, has another Park exhibit — a small marine museum which is housed in what were once the lighthouse keeper's quarters. The tower of the light is a very old one. It originally stood for many years on the south coast of England, but when it was replaced with a new one there, it was brought to Newfoundland, to be erected here at Rocky Harbour in 1897. It is now operated automatically, but for all of its first seventy-three years on this site, it was served by only three light keepers, two of whom were father and son.

Rocky Harbour has a remarkable piece of natural granite sculpture that was found on the shore some years ago. Its shape, smoothly carved by the sea into three elegant flanges, suggests the propeller of a large ship. It stands in the middle of the community, appropriate symbol of the town's name, its boat-building tradition, and its dependence on the sea.

When the boat-building yards at Rocky Harbour were at the height of their production, a friend and I once had a curious and rather charming experience concerning one of their longliners. We had planned a leisurely trip to the tip of the Great Northern Peninsula, exploring the many little fishing places along the way. On the stocks at Gordon Shears' shipyard in Rocky Harbour, we noticed a handsome new longliner all but ready for the sea. We stopped to look at her and wondered idly what little harbour was to be her home port.

Down the coast (for that is the way north is in Newfoundland) the fishery was in full swing. Every cove and harbour, every little niche in the coastline, was busy with boats and purposeful men.

Sunday morning found us driving northward round the shore of St. Barbe Bay with a heavy southwest wind whipping the sea into white rollers, spray flying from their crests. Across the windswept bay a settlement stood out on the northern point, its houses startlingly white on the green turf and not a tree to break the force of the onshore wind. It looked a bleak and uncompromising spot. The community was Anchor Point and a short spur led into it from the highway. In the tiny cut into the coastline that served as harbour was the finest fleet of longliners we had ever seen and on this galey Sunday morning, no less than eleven lay tossing at the wharves as though straining to get out and on with the job. Boats and wharves alike had a neat and finished look that reflected the pride and care of their owners. Most of them, we learned, were fairly new and all belonged to local men. As we stood by the harbour admiring the little fleet, a spry elderly lady stopped by for a chat. Her eyes gleamed with pride as we admired the boats. Names were soon exchanged and a lively conversation was going on by the time we strolled by her home. Impulsively, and with great glee, she said, "Come in! Come in, now, and see the name!" Knowing no less than three ways in which her name is spelt in Newfoundland, we thought she just wanted to make sure we had it right. But no! As we entered her gleaming kitchen she called to her husky fisherman son, "Fetch the name, boy, fetch the name!", which sent him hustling off to a small back room while we stood mystified, waiting to see what he would bring. He emerged, beaming with pride, bearing the beautifully painted bow and stern nameplates of a vessel, the *Anchor Point North*, his father's new longliner. "She's being built at Shears' in Rocky Harbour and she's all ready bar the shaft," his mother explained. Intrigued at the coincidence, we told her of the longliner we had seen there. "That's her!" she said, "Painted white and grey was she? That's our *Anchor Point North*. That's our longliner!" The whole family glowed with pride to think we had actually seen and noticed their new boat. Their joy and pride were infectious and we promised to look even more closely at her on the way home.

Back at Rocky Harbour a few days later, we stopped to look again at the boat on the stocks, now shining with her last coats of paint. As we looked up at the sturdy line of her bow, there, firmly screwed in place, were the neat red letters *Anchor Point North*. Our friends had already claimed her as their own!

Norris Point

The road linking Rocky Harbour with Norris Point climbs toward a ridge, and as one drives up this six-mile stretch one encounters a panoramic view of the Long Range Mountains. The long chain of rounded hills and steep valleys reflect the day's weather and are an ever-changing landscape. In early summer the mountains are all brilliant colours in the sun and splotched with flying cloud shadows. Under leaden skies they recede in endless shades of grey as the mist and rainstorms drift among them. Winter sees their glistening white change in the westering sun to lemon and to gold, and as the sun sets, to pink, rose, purple, and so to the indigo of night.

Just a little way over the ridge, the whole of Bonne Bay suddenly spreads before you in a view that has been famous since long before anyone thought of a national park in western Newfoundland. The little town that spreads over the land just below is Norris Point, in reality a cluster of quite distinct little communities. Wild Cove, a lovely little green cove that basks in the last rays of the setting sun, faces due west and takes all the pounding of the Gulf of St. Lawrence. Neddy Harbour, which has spread in recent years all along its land-locked inlet, and Bugden's Lane, just a loop of road near the beaches, are two other miniature communities. But the true Norris Point is the point of land across the water from the peninsula of Gadd's Harbour, and through this narrow tickle flow all the tides of the Main Arm of Bonne Bay. The highway winds its way for about a mile through the town, past the Cottage Hospital, over a narrow peninsula, and down to the dock in the shelter of the point.

The names Neddy and Norris both belonged to Neddy Norris, a shadowy character who came and went before the ancestors of today's residents. He was well known to the few Micmac Indians who lived there at the time, and they spoke of him to the newcomers. Somehow his two names stuck, and are perhaps the only things he left behind.

The first English settlers were William Humber and his wife. They arrived from Dorset in 1833 and were for many years the only English inhabitants. The next to arrive were the Hardings. The story goes that they had set out from the south coast where they lived to move to Codroy near the southwest tip of the Island, but a violent storm blew their boat out to sea. When, after many days at sea, they eventually made land they found themselves in Bonne Bay. As they planned to spend the summers fishing off the Labrador, the location suited them well and they stayed.

Attracted by the ready market for salt cod and the profitable herring and lobster fisheries, the population steadily increased. Trapping for fur provided an additional income for some of the settlers, and during the First World War a fox farm was set up to supply fur for pilots' flying suits.

In recent years the population of Norris Point has risen sharply due to the relocation of families from some of the smaller communities within the Park area and the number of Park employees who now live there. The town now has more than a thousand inhabitants.

Norris Point is a natural port, and through the centuries, while Newfoundland was a British Colony, British naval ships called in on regular patrols. The square-rigged men o' war must have been a splendid sight sailing into the bay. With its deep water, sheltered anchorages and friendly people, Norris Point was a favourite port of call for the ships, and one where they would spend several days taking on supplies and water and giving the crew a run ashore.

An enterprising businessman, John Harding, offered to supply the Navy on a regular basis with coal, which he imported from Cape Breton, and with fresh meat and bread. This was the start of a useful and profitable relationship that lasted for many years until the naval patrols ceased. The places where the naval vessels used to anchor, or run a hawser ashore in those early days, are still well known landmarks for local people.

Safe anchorages were, and still are, a necessity, for Bonne Bay is well known for the tearing winds that funnel down between the mountains. A northeaster is the most dreaded wind in Norris Point, and has been known to carry away whole buildings — including an almost-completed church in 1943. Just a few years ago, a house was blown apart and its roof, together with a motley array of household debris, sailed across the bay to land on the shore in Curzon Village. Luckily the family had taken refuge in the basement and no one was hurt.

From the time of the first settlers until the Second World War medical services were either totally lacking or, at best, minimal. Between the wars one overworked doctor tried to serve the whole Bonne Bay area. The privations of the Depression years added to the health problems with which he had to deal, and births, deaths, illnesses and accidents were the preoccupation of all. Minor surgery had to be done on kitchen tables and people with more serious troubles had to travel to St. John's by coastal boat. All nursing fell to mothers and other family members. Death from all manner of causes was familiar to everyone, and the loss of children in infancy, mothers in childbirth, and anyone from pneumonia or tuberculosis — the most dreaded illness and a scourge all through those years — was an all too common occurrence. The building of the Cottage Hospital at Norris Point in 1939 brought proper medical facilities to the area for the first time. The construction work brought some welcome employment, and the permanent jobs the hospital provided helped the struggling local economy.

A few roads began to be built during the war years, replacing the old trails and cart tracks. As soon as there were just a few miles of road linking neighbouring settlements the first car arrived, delivered by coastal steamer. Gazing at it with awe and wonder, few could imagine a day when every household would have one. That one would eventually drive to St. Anthony in five hours or to St. John's in ten would have seemed like a crazy dream!

News of the outside world was always scanty. Passing travellers and vessels brought news from up and down the coast. From further afield news came by telegraph or in the weekly mail. With the war came the first radios, big wooden boxes with a train of heavy glass batteries. With only one or two in the community, most people heard the news secondhand from those privileged to listen.

For the youngsters, the outside world that you could hear and smell and touch was the coastal steamer that called every two weeks. As it blew to announce its coming, people flocked to the wharf — some to collect freight they had ordered, others to meet a friend travelling down the coast, but most, including all the children, just for the fun and excitement of it all. Despite increasing sophistication over the years, the arrival of the coastal boat in Norris Point, as in all other small communities, remained a source of news, interest, and fun until their visits ceased when roads made their service obsolete.

A coastal boat still calls at Norris Point in the spring and the fall, for each year a number of fishing families from around the Bonne Bay area take ship for Labrador, carrying with them their fishing boat and gear and all the household goods they need to spend the summer months fishing off the Labrador coast. The ship's lifeboats are stowed on deck and every davit carries a fishing boat instead. The coastal boat brings them home again in time to take part in the local fall fishery.

Neddy Hill

Close by the dock at Norris Point is a little hill called Neddy Hill. Just 250 feet high, it is one of those small hummocks, surrounded by mountains, that can give one such spectacular views. The community built a trail around its crown some years ago, and for a quick orientation early in your stay in Gros Morne, or for anyone who can't manage long hikes, it is a wonderfully rewarding little climb.

The trail starts from the parking lot by the dock, follows a little lane and, beside an old fish store built over the shore, starts steeply up the hill. Soon you find some rough wooden steps, and once at the top of these you have done most of the climbing. The trail, with ups and downs, wooded sections and well-placed gaps in the trees, gives you a full circle of splendid views.

The first outlook is back over the Tickle, toward Gadd's Harbour and Shag Cliff. Across the open water of the main part of the bay is the beautiful Western Arm with the tableland as backdrop, bare rusty rock, pock-marked with snow till late in the summer.

Almost the whole of the eight mile length of the Main Arm can be seen, with Killdevil, the boldly striped mountain at its far end. Passing through a belt of thick trees, an opening gives you a fine view of Gros Morne and its smaller neighbour, Crow Cliff. From here you are looking at the side of Gros Morne that you will climb if you hike the James Callahan trail.

From the west end of Neddy Hill you can see almost the whole of the community and look down into tranquil Neddy Harbour where boats and yachts are usually at anchor. Soon you come out onto an open grassy area and find that you have made almost a full circle and can look out of the mouth of Bonne Bay to the Gulf of St. Lawrence. A high rock stack is conspicuous on the skyline of the south cliffs. Known as The Old Man, it has been a landmark for mariners all through the ages. To return to your car, you can either scramble down the steep bank below you, or take a short cut over the top of the hill and return by the path you climbed.

As well as having this extraordinary round of views, Neddy Hill is usually lively with bird song and you could see any or all of a dozen species there. Just to hike the trail takes little more than half an hour, but with your maps, binoculars and camera in hand you may be tempted to spend a couple of hours there and use up quite a bit of film!

Gadd's Harbour and Shag Cliff

Across the Tickle is the beautiful little peninsula and sheltered cove of Gadd's Harbour. Thick woods and steep hills surround a saddle of green meadow. On either side of the peninsula are beaches; the outer one, continually pounded by the force of the prevailing wind and sea, is piled with driftwood; the inner one is protected within a deep, horseshoe-shaped cove.

Just across the Tickle from Norris Point are the idyllic green coves of Gadd's Harbour, once a tiny community.

A generation ago Gadd's Harbour had a small community, and on that fertile ground the livyers were very self-sufficient, raising vegetables and fruit trees, sheep, cattle and ponies. But eventually the inconvenience of having to cross by boat or over the ice for school, church, social contacts and provisions must have persuaded them to move across to Norris Point.

Just to the south of Gadd's Harbour are steep and rugged bluffs with rocky pinnacles projecting above the forest. Certain old spruce here are favourite perches for the bald eagles whose brilliant white heads and tails catch your eye among the dark green of the woods. The beach below, Long Beach, has an astonishing array of small, multicoloured pebbles, all rounded by the endless surf.

Toward the Main Arm the deep cove is dominated by Shag Cliff. Its light grey shale is made up of millions of sedimented layers, tip-tilted to stand almost vertical. On a day of contrasting light, this beautiful pale cliff can look almost luminous. Some of the most ancient of trilobite fossils have been found in this area.

This idyllic little harbour is accessible only by small boat, and several times we have sailed or canoed across, for it is a magical place on a calm evening. With a driftwood fire on the beach, we've watched the sun set over the mouth of the Bay. On one memorable evening, with a low-lying bank of fog out at sea, the round disc of the sun went through extraordinary distortions as it set, becoming, in turn, a sort of blazing box with a lid, then something like an urn, until finally, as a flattened bowl, it touched the horizon and gradually sank out of sight.

CHAPTER 8

The Tuckamore Shore

Baker's Brook

Not many years ago there was a tiny fishing community at Baker's Brook, sharing its name with the Brook. The community lay on the shore to the south of the river mouth and drew what shelter was to be had from the tuckamore, the wind-flattened trees of that exposed bit of coast. The shelving, rocky shore was good lobstering ground, and the spring lobster season was the main fishery of the year.

Although the community was small, lacking in amenities and bleak in the eyes of strangers, it had a character all its own. To the people who lived there, Baker's Brook was, above all else, their own land by right of long tenure. They were proud and self-sufficient people in many ways, but it was impossible for the government to provide so small a place with modern amenities. And so, when the Park came and wanted the land without the inhabitants, the provincial government agreed to the people being relocated.

The Park was not ungenerous in its compensation and each of the families was given a new house and land in the place of their choice. For the most part, the people chose Rocky Harbour or Norris Point. While the young people benefitted most from the move, the older generation mourned the loss of their own land. The fishermen, meanwhile, could still use their old boat ramps and fishing premises, travelling back and forth in their trucks.

Most of the people of Baker's Brook were Deckers, descendents of one of the earliest settlers in the district. As a family, the Deckers had, and still have, the reputation of never being at a loss for words, or for a reply to any challenge, and there is a story that has become part of the folklore of the area. The government of the day was seeking to improve the quality of the sheep in the outports and offered to supply purebred rams to improve the existing stock. Tom Decker, the patriarch of the family at that time, sent in an application for a ram for Baker's Brook. To his disgust he received the reply that the small number of people in his community did not qualify them to receive a ram. He wrote back in fury, saying that he didn't want a ram for his *people* but for his *sheep*! In the end, he got one!

The little settlement lay in the path of all who travelled the coast, for the strip of open ground along the back of the beaches that served as footpath, cart-track, and dogteam trail was the only trail from time immemorial until the highway was first built in the 1950s. From Baker's Brook you can walk north or south for miles on this stretch of grass and gravel. Occasionally it plunges through a cutting in the tuck, and where there are cliffs it follows the top of them. Besides being an exilarating seaside walk, these old tracks are interesting to explore and the experience brings home to one the isolation of the small communities and the distances people had to walk even to reach the next little settlement. Walking there, one comes to realize too the importance that each and every traveller must have had as the only carrier of news in those times.

Along the tidewash, tidal pools among the rocks are an endless source of interest and entertainment. Each pool is a world in miniature; plants wave in constant motion, while among them the minute sea creatures go about their business and prey upon each other. Driftwood lines the crest of the beach and shelters a wealth of beach plants, growing somehow out of the bed of rocks and pebbles.

Behind the beach the trees are matted and flattened by the prevailing on-shore winds. This belt of tuckamore provided welcome shelter for the sheep which used to wander everywhere before the establishment of the Park. It too is a microcosm and has its own community of small creatures such as mice, voles, weasels and birds. On some parts of the coast, instead of trees there are large areas of bog, and on them one can gather marshberries in the fall. Being close kin to cranberries, they make delicious jam or sauce for turkey. They are often numerous, but are very hard to see as their varied colours match so closely the mosses, plants and peat of the bog.

Baker's Brook Pond, out of which flows Baker's Brook, lies in another of the steep clefts in the Long Range. Deep in the woods are a series of lovely waterfalls, and in 1985 the Park opened a new hiking trail that takes you to them. The trail starts from

Deep in the woods are the Baker's Brook Falls.

the Park's main campground at the foot of Berry Hill. It is distinctive among the many trails of Gros Morne as it runs through wet, low-lying terrain rich in wetland wildflowers. In early July these are at their best. Soon after the start of the trail, showy lady's slipper orchids grow in an open grove of young larches; marsh marigolds and scent-bottle orchids (ladies tresses) are found in many of the wet places; and great drifts of purple iris grow thickly in slow-moving boggy streams. In the woods, bunch-berry flowers line the trail and the scent of twin-flower hangs in the air.

The trail passes a beaver pond where frogs can be heard croaking all summer long. Frogs have only recently appeared in this part of the Island, having apparently spread across from eastern Newfoundland where they are quite common.

Long before you reach the falls, you hear the roar of water. The river tumbles over a series of ridges in a rushing torrent, sending up clouds of spray and mist. The two main falls and the stretch of swirling river between them can best be seen from the viewpoint at the end of the trail.

The Baker's Brook trail in winter makes a very pleasant cross-country ski run for it is fairly level and much of it is sheltered in the woods. The falls, when stilled by ice, are as impressive as they are in summer.

Berry Head Pond

About halfway between the two campgrounds of Berry Hill and Green Point is a pond near the highway called Berry Head Pond. A specially-built trail leads to it and along the near side, making the pond accessible for disabled people and wheelchair users.

On a fine summer evening it is a lovely place to spend an hour or two watching the beavers which often appear there for an evening feed and a swim. By keeping still and quiet, I watched one feeding just four or five yards away and, with binoculars, could see every movement of his small and dextrous paws. Twiddling his twig at lightning speed, he stripped it clean in seconds and reached for another one, his actions a comic caricature of our own when eating corn on the cob!

There were two beaver houses on the pond at that time, and from the trail that goes around the far side of the pond I watched two pairs of beavers idly cruising around. Only the gently moving Vs of their wakes disturbed the glassy water. Beyond the black silhouette of the trees, the westering sun lit up the sky and the still pond reflected all the blazing colours of its setting.

Green Point

A favourite with many of Gros Morne's regular visitors, Green Point campground neatly fits into the natural environment of wind-beaten tuckamore that lines the coast. Although it boasts no showers or fancy facilities, it is the place to spend a few nights if you want to sleep with the sound of the sea and the smell of the salty wind and the tuckamore. To set up your tent close to the sheltering tuck and to sit on the low cliff top watching the waves beat on the rounded boulders below while the sun sets over the Gulf is to experience something of the essence of the northwest coast.

The campground lies just south of the grassy point of land where the small fishing settlement of Green Point was located. The rocky point gave shelter from the north wind and in this shelter the fishermen cleared a sort of lagoon, with a ring of boulders to protect their small boats. There was good land on the point, and once the settlers cleared the trees they grew vegetables and raised the animals they needed. But here again the community was too small to be viable, and when the Park was established the families were relocated to larger settlements. Only the fishing premises were allowed to remain.

The low cliff that forms the point consists of millions of sedimented layers of rock, some paper thin, some an inch thick and patterned like sand ripples at low tide. It is a remarkable demonstration of a geological time span, for these millions of layers have been tilted up so that now they stand on edge and one can follow them along the cliff till they disappear below the turf. The sea takes its toll on the point with every storm, gradually eroding the layers and revealing their multiplicity of colours, patterns and textures.

Sally's Cove

I used to look upon Sally's Cove as being extraordinarily bleak and unprotected, even for this rugged coast, and wondered for a long time why people had settled there, and why they stayed to cope with such tough conditions. In the Park's original plan, Sally's Cove, like several other small communities, was marked for expropriation. When the people put up a staunch resistance, and received support that amounted to a major demonstration at the time of the Park's inauguration, I still could not see why they were so determined to cling to this exposed bit of coast.

I can't pinpoint the change in my feelings, but somehow I have come to understand just what land means to its owners, here and everywhere. The territorial instinct, so profound and universal, is something we share with the whole animal kingdom. It seems to have little to do with quality or location, but is intimately bound up with family, with heritage, with our sense of belonging, and is basic to our self-esteem. So it is small wonder that, where several generations have wrested a livelihood from the sea and the land — as they have at Sally's Cove — the bond between a family and its land goes beyond mere ownership. In a very real sense, they are a part of the land, and the land a part of them. I look at Sally's Cove differently now, seeing not just its bleakness but its assets, those it still has and, even more, those it had before its life was radically changed by being surrounded by a national park.

Although there is no semblance of a natural harbour, a shallow point breaks some of the force of the sea. On the rocky beach, the fishermen build a particularly substantial type of ramp, unique to Sally's Cove, that withstands the pounding of the sea. Using their trucks, they haul their flat-bottomed boats up, out of reach of the waves. It is the proximity of the good lobstering grounds that makes it worth all the trouble of creating a little fishing harbour where none existed. It also accounts for the enormous stacks of lobster pots that stand as high as the fishermen's sheds once the lobstering season is over.

Behind the beach, the level land provides ample space for homes, gardens, hay fields and the pasture that was needed to raise the many sheep and ponies that were so essential to life there in times past. On the broad coastal plain, belts of trees divide the bogs, and close to the mountains there is fine forest cover. From the plain, the woods and the mountains the settlers could get all they needed of berries, firewood, saw-logs and game, both large and small, for meat and for the furs that supplemented their sparse incomes.

One oldtimer tells of his years as a young man when he would be out with the dawn in his boat to haul a couple of hundred lobster pots. After a late second breakfast, he would head for the hills with his gun and be back in the afternoon with a caribou. There were no game laws then, nor were there snowmobiles and all-terrain vehicles, but people were few, caribou were plentiful, and nature kept its balance.

Now all the land around is Park; hunting is no longer permitted and wood-cutting is tightly controlled. But times have changed in other ways too. A cash economy has made subsistence activities less essential and, since most families have a truck, they are no longer dependent on hunting close to home.

Just a few years ago a great many ponies and sheep grazed the long meadow along the road all summer long. The ponies hauled logs in winter and the sheep provided meat and wool. The sheep, whose ancestors must have come over with the first settlers, are of no known breed. Many are a beautiful brown or black and their fleeces make the handsome mottled yarn so much used for knitting fishermen's guernseys. The sheep stock has been much improved in recent years by the introduction of pedigree rams. Ponies have given way to snowmobiles, and because of the high-speed traffic on the roads both sheep and ponies are now confined to pastures and much reduced in numbers. One still misses the herds of sleek and idle ponies that used to wander everywhere in summertime, and the sheep grazing on the cliff tops.

Fortunately for the people of Sally's Cove, Parks Canada changed their minds about phasing out the community and decided to make it another Park enclave instead. Unfortunately, however, this decision was not made before many had been persuaded to move by the offer of a new house in a larger community. The little settlement is much reduced in size now, and one feels sorry that those who remain have lost so many of their old neighbours.

If you live in a place like Sally's Cove, the harshness of travel in the old days, by boat or dogteam but most often on foot, is a memory that dies hard, even in this age of comfortable vehicles. The traditional hospitality of the west coast stems from the experience of travelling and travellers in days gone by. For, not so long ago, every journey was rough and hazardous. The traveller at the door inevitably arrived cold, tired, hungry and footsore, and whoever he or she was, would be welcomed, fed with the best available, and given a bed for the night. With the thin population, everyone knew or knew of everyone else, and most people had relatives up and down the three hundred miles of the northwest coast. The news exchanged with the traveller in the lamp-lit kitchen was the thread that kept everyone in touch with each other. Every human life was precious, and health and safety were everyone's concern for they had no one to rely on but each other.

Not only in Sally's Cove, but in every little community, the traditional hospitality still holds good and accounts for the generous spread that is put before the stranger who accepts the invitation to "come in and have a cup of tea!"

CHAPTER 9

Western Brook Pond

A Fish-Shaped Bit of Blue

Arriving in Newfoundland from almost anywhere, most of us think of a pond as a small pool near a farmstead where horses drink and ducks paddle, or perhaps a little frog pond in a shady hollow. Once we set foot in Newfoundland our ideas have to change, for here only the grandest bodies of water are lakes and nearly all the rest, both great and small, are ponds.

And so it is that Western Brook Pond is the modest name of the most dramatic piece of terrain in the Island, if not in Eastern Canada. It is an immense body of water, twelve miles long, lying in a cleft that runs deep into the Long Range Mountains at one of their highest points. The mountains are split as though with an axe, and the two thousand foot cliffs drop sheer into the pond to a fathomless depth below the black water.

The brook flowing out of it is a sizeable salmon stream which winds diagonally across the coastal plain and spreads into a series of ponds and steadies along the way. The road bridge crosses Western Brook just before it twists sharply through high sand dunes and flows across a sandy beach to the sea. The trail to Western Brook Pond was the first one to be built by the Park, and a boat tour opened up this wonderful fresh water fjord to the public in the early 1970s.

It is impossible not to be thrilled by a trip through the gorge, and every time I go, taking my summer visitors for the highlight of their stay, the weather or the quality of light is different, or I see something I haven't seen before. But never again can I recapture the magic of that first trip by canoe! Gliding silently, making scarcely a ripple, hearing every sound, we touched the smooth vertical granite with our fingers and looked into the still depths of the clear dark water. Tiny and vulnerable, we knew ourselves to be at the mercy of the elements and on no more than equal terms with the world of nature around us.

I first became aware of Western Brook Pond in 1959 while fishing for sea trout at the mouth of Western Brook. A splendid sunset lit up the mountains and the jagged cliffs of the gorge, and I wondered how one could get a close look at them. The river warden told me how to get to the shore of the pond, but said that the gorge itself was inaccessible except by boat. A canoe was the only kind of boat one could hope to take up the river, but it seemed a fragile craft in which to venture into the gorge which is notorious for violent wind squalls.

Having neither a canoe nor a suitable companion with whom to attempt the trip, Western Brook Pond remained a dream for many years, and every time I looked at the map of Newfoundland my eyes would wander to that fish-shaped bit of blue half way up the west coast. By 1967, however, I had acquired a canoe, and a good deal of experience in using it, and my companion on many weekend trips on lakes and rivers had caught my enthusiasm for exploring Western Brook Pond. So, in late June we took a few days leave to make the attempt.

A 450 mile drive across the Island brought us to the mouth of Western Brook on a beautiful sunny day. We sought out the river warden and his friend the storekeeper, who were both very familiar with the river. The idea of anyone using a canoe was strange to them as these are not much used by Newfoundlanders. That anyone would trouble to go up the river for any reason but to fish clearly made little sense to them. That this effort should be undertaken by two women must have been beyond all reason! As they answered our numerous questions about portages and the state of the river, their doubts seemed lulled a little, but their expressions told us that you wouldn't catch either one of them putting his foot in a canoe!

One fact was all too clear: the river was very high after recent heavy rains and might well give us trouble. We did not have time to wait for more ideal conditions, and so decided to try it anyway. With our gear carefully stowed and lashed, we set out in the early afternoon. The first half mile gave us good paddling up a deep, reed-lined section, but once out of this a heavy current forced us to start wading and towing the canoe. The water from the deep mountain lake was very cold.

All afternoon we kept going doggedly. The river was as much as a foot above normal in places and the banks and bushes were partly submerged. We passed the first big steady, Gull Steady, but were too weary to tackle the particularly bad section of river above it. It wasn't much of a place to spend the night, but we made camp in the shelter of a few stunted larches.

Even from the highway, the cliffs of Western Brook Pond are vast and impressive.

Next morning was grey and cold, the water icy and the rushing torrent not appreciably less than it had been the day before. We knew there should be a portage but, search as we would, could find nothing resembling a trail. Before long the inevitable happened: as we struggled to manoeuver round a jam of logs and boulders, the canoe slewed momentarily across the current, dipped her bow quarter, and swamped. A paddle shot off downstream, its owner in pursuit but unable to keep up. Meanwhile, the canoe itself was in danger from the pressure of water jamming it against a boulder. Although we lost several bundles of gear, we had to ignore them while we emptied the canoe.

With the canoe eventually lying safely in a small backwater, we took a tally of the remaining soggy bundles and found three vital ones missing: the tent, one sleeping bag, and the cooking gear. We went downstream to search for them, and for the precious paddle, but none of them turned up. Although it seemed unlikely, with so many rocks to stop them, we figured they must have floated on down to Gull Steady.

By now we knew we had to abandon the attempt and go back. We were cold and disappointed; the canoe was heavy with wet kit; and a stick was a poor substitute for the bow paddle. We crept downstream, searching all the way for the lost gear and reached the landing place without seeing any of it. We were completely puzzled by its disappearance and, feeling rather foolish, even searched along the seashore at the mouth of the river!

Although we couldn't take the canoe up again, we were determined at least to see the gorge from the shore of the pond. So early next morning we walked in the way the fishermen go to the trout pools. There was no real path, just an occasional stick poked into the marsh which might — or might not — mark the way. Squelching across the bogs, pushing through scrub, and, for much of the way, wading in the river itself, we eventually reached the pond.

The great cliffs reared up before us. Even across the four miles of open water, we felt dwarfed by their height and realized, even more clearly than before, that getting into the gorge and up its eight mile length was going to be a formidable task.

This long and tiresome walk proved to be a most valuable reconnaissance for the second trip up river with the canoe, but meanwhile it had an unexpected result: we found the obscure portage trail past the site of the previous day's mishap. Tired as we were, we dropped down through the woods to take another look at the place where the canoe had swamped. There, in a back eddy, just where we reached the river, we saw with absolute astonishment first one, then another green plastic bundle — the missing tent and sleeping bag! The absurdity of our forlorn search along the seashore while the bundles were not twenty yards from the capsize sent us into gales of laughter as we leapt from rock to rock looking for the rucksack. In no time we found it, wedged against a rock in mid-stream immediately below the log jam. And there, just below the spot where it was last seen racing toward the sea, was the paddle, resting against a log!

What finally brought our helpless laughter to a halt was the effort to lift the water-logged tent and sleeping bag up the steep bank to the trail. The bundles must have weighed a hundred pounds apiece, and even when we had wrung out all the water we could they were still enormously heavy. And the wet army rucksack was no light weight either! While thoroughly daunted at the thought of carrying all this the remaining two miles to the road, we were determined not to have to make a second trip. Somehow we loaded it all on our backs and tottered the last soggy stretch to the car.

And so ended our attempt to realize the dream. At that time there seemed little likelihood that we would have a second chance.

The failure of the first attempt only served to increase the challenge. Many were the winter evenings when the conversation would slip around to Western Brook. Out

Rocky Harbour Cove, with Gros Morne to the far right.

Shag Cliff, its steep shale catching the light.

A peaceful evening at Gadd's Harbour.

In Norris Point, a lane leads to Neddy Hill, a small hill with a circuit of splendid views.

Sparkling water on the Main Arm of Bonne Bay.

Sally's Cove and its rugged and windswept shore. Once threatened with expropriation, it is now a Park enclave community.

The uniquely-designed boat ramps of Sally's Cove withstand the pounding sea.

The great gorge of Western Brook Pond.

A fairy-tale waterfall on Western Brook Pond.

The stream was a rushing cascade as we approached the vast slab of smooth grey granite.

Exploring the cliff tops of Western Brook Pond, I found the top of the familiar gully.

The cliff edges were as sharp and sudden as the sides of a box.

The community of St. Paul's and the rugged mountains of the Long Range.

Ponies graze on the Cow Head Peninsula.

Sand engulfs the trees at Shallow Bay, leaving silver skeletons among the dunes.

Sunset lights the pink scree of the crumbling ridge at Parsons Pond.

The steep sides were identically mirrored and met at water level like the beaks of two huge birds.

The multicoloured beach rocks reflect the varied geology of the region.

would come the maps and diaries and always we'd chuckle over the memory of the bundles revolving slowly in an eddy while we searched five miles away along the shore!

As things turned out, the following year found us there again. With a lot more canoeing experience behind us, we planned and packed carefully for a four-day expedition. Everything was stowed in strong plastic bags. A spare paddle and all the gear were tightly lashed in, and we carried not an ounce of extra weight. The replacements for last year's ruined camera and binoculars were in a tightly-sealed container, ready to hand. Despite our hearty respect for this vast and rugged terrain, with the canoe lying trim and level by the bank, the weather clear, and the river neither too high nor too low, we felt we had a good chance of getting all the way in to the gorge this time.

Before leaving, we dropped in to the little store by the bridge where we received a warm welcome from the storekeeper's wife. Her husband was upriver, fishing. We told her our plans, and when to expect us down again. Then, without further delay, we set out.

Knowing the river now, we had little difficulty picking the best route up the tricky stretches or finding the obscure portage. We were paddling hard up a beautiful tree-lined stretch when we came upon the storekeeper, fishing from a big rock overlooking a trout pool. He nearly dropped his rod in surprise when he saw us, but greeted us with "Is yous de women who was up here last year?" We stopped to tell him our plans before paddling on upstream.

As we came out onto Long Steady, the last of the three steadies on the way upriver, we came upon a family of black duck — mother and eight ducklings. In their alarm they sped off up the steady and, though we tried not to frighten them, they paddled at top speed the whole way ahead of us. The ducklings could not dive as their mother clearly wanted them to do, but swam with enormous energy, sometimes churning up the water as they almost ran on the surface.

It was a moment of real triumph when we paddled out at last onto the open water of the pond, still and splendid in the evening sun. We made for a sandy peninsula opposite the mouth of the gorge and set up camp. As we ate our supper by the fire, we watched an aerobatic display by various small birds, hunting flies over the water; kinglets, swallows and fly-catchers, each performing in its characteristic way and enjoying a feast of flies.

Peering out of the tent early next morning we saw with dismay that the weather was very threatening. Bands of black water advanced out of the gorge and, as the wind hit us, a few whitecaps broke from the rising waves. We could not venture into the gorge that day but decided to cross to the north shore, from which we would have a shorter distance to paddle into the mouth of the gorge when the wind dropped. It was a rough but exhilarating paddle, quartering carefully so as not to get either bow or beam directly into the waves.

As we made camp on a small pebble beach, the wind swung to the southeast — the worst wind in these parts — and towards evening rose to a full gale. Our tent was only a few feet from the pounding waves on the shore, and many times in the night we had to pile more rocks on those already holding the guy-ropes and the lashings of the canoe. Never have I spent a noisier night, for our little nylon tent flapped and cracked like a hundred flags!

We were tent-bound by driving rain much of the next day and began to fear that our time would run out before we could see the gorge. Studying the map we figured we might at least be able to look down into it if we could climb the mountains on the north side. As the next day was still too windy to use the canoe, we set out to climb by way of a small watercourse, the only route through the impenetrable scrub. But when, after many hours, we came out into the open we found that the way ahead was no easier and we were no more than a third of the way to the top. It was disappointing to have to turn back, but at least we were rewarded with a marvelous view of the coast. The whole coastal plain spread before us and, with maps and binoculars, we could pick out every feature from the mouth of Bonne Bay in the south to Parsons Pond in the north.

By now the sun was blazing down and, as we made our way back down the innumerable bends of the stream, we felt more hopeful of good weather the next day. On the way a fish hawk (osprey) swooped and shrieked at us for being too near her nest, a six foot construction of twigs that crowned a tall dead spruce at the foot of a waterfall. We wondered how such a precarious structure could have survived the gale.

Back at our camp on the pebble beach, the wind had dropped to a gentle breeze. A golden sunset lit the cliffs, and the last few shreds of cloud drifted among the mountain tops. As we ate our supper in the afterglow, the eerie call of the loons rang out across the water. We dared to hope that we would get into the gorge next day.

The morning dawned still and clear and we set off at last for the mouth of the gorge. The loons were there again, rending the morning stillness with their cries. A flight of ducks rose and wheeled away to land with scudding feet at a safe distance.

With a light breeze behind us, we paddled steadily and fast, passing the mile-wide mouth of the gorge in about an hour. Hugging the north shore, the two thousand foot cliffs seemed to hang over us. It made one dizzy to look up at them. Here and there a gully had formed where huge rock falls had smashed down and lay at the steepest possible angle, continuing on down into the depths as far as one could see.

Where the cliffs were not too steep, the sides of the gorge were lush with vegetation. From a distance we had taken this green cover to be a bushy growth of alder and birch, but such was the scale of the place that we now saw that they were big forest trees. The woods rang with a continuous chorus of small birds — warblers, white-throats, chickadees, kinglets — and every sound echoed from cliff to cliff across the half mile of water. Our attention was arrested by a glorious flow of song from a Newfoundland winter wren, proclaiming his territory from the top of some tall tree. Several times he treated us to a burst of loud sweet music, five or ten seconds of intensely varied song, unbelievable from so minute a breast.

Approaching the big point on the north side, the wind switched suddenly and blew in our faces. As we rounded this great bastion of rock we saw for the first time the inner part of the gorge, and the south cliffs revealed in their full splendour. We had seen, even from the road, their jagged tops against the sky; now they towered above us. For nearly a mile, the cliffs dropped almost sheer into the water, the vast slabs of grey seamed here and there by dykes that ran from top to bottom. Here, the great cleaving axe had cut clean; the cliff faces were square to the level mountain tops and hardly a crevice broke their knife-edges against the sky.

Here we took careful stock of our situation. This is no place to be caught out on the water, for any strong wind funnels through the gorge in fierce, battering squalls. There are only the steep rock-falls to go ashore on if the need arises, uncomfortable and exposed places on which to sit out a gale. We had another six miles to go to reach the head of the pond, then twelve miles back to the river outlet, and five or six winding miles down river to the landing — all to be covered by evening. We pressed on as fast as we could, keeping a wary eye on the weather.

High up on the north side, a waterfall tumbled white through a notch, draining one of the high ponds in the mountains. It disappeared completely into a scree of boulders, not to be seen again. The course of another stream, falling through wildly jagged clefts and crannies, could be traced all the way down the cliff, finally to fall some fifty feet directly into the water — a fairy tale waterfall. Crowning the last bend on the south side, an immense rock castle stood guard over a deep and thickly-wooded gully in which we could hear the roar of an unseen cataract.

As we rounded the last bend we could see, finally, all the way in to the far end of the gorge. But our time was running out and we could go no further. We tied up the canoe and scrambled onto the top of a flat boulder by the shore. Tantalized by the view, and disappointed not to be able to go all the way in, we spread out the map and examined every feature of the place with binoculars. Over the last cliffs on the south side a thin waterfall was blown to a mist by the wind. Beyond the head of the pond the valley was flanked by wildly rugged crags, the steep V between them sloping up to a high notch at the top.

Rugged crags and a waterfall blown to a mist by the wind at the east end of Western Brook Pond.

After a quick bite of lunch, we turned resolutely back. For several miles a steady breeze followed us. As we were tired with paddling and had quite a distance to go, we made an effective sail out of a rain jacket supported by two of the paddles and sailed gently along, our eyes feasting on the scenery around us. But long before we reached the open part of the pond we saw the now familiar and threatening dark streak of water advancing through the mouth of the gorge. The wind had changed again and the paddles were soon delving and thrusting against wind and waves. Crossing the open water to the distant river outlet was tedious and tiring, and we were glad to reach the easy, downstream canoeing of Western Brook.

After the day of dramatic scenery in the gorge, the tranquil sections of the meandering river were like the slow movement of a symphony, a time of peace and reflection as we threaded our way down the reed-lined waterways. On Long Steady we met again the family of ducks. They too had spent three days acquiring new experiences for the strongest duckling had now learned to dive, and did so whenever his mother did. Quite suddenly, the other seven ducklings decided to try as well and plopped under, to emerge again almost at once, shaking the water from their coats of down. Obviously delighted with their new skill, they plopped up and down repeatedly, encouraged by much quacking from their mother. This time we drifted quietly by without frightening them.

At the portage we met the river warden and his friend. (The first I saw of them was the warden's big boots as I struggled up the steep bank with the first bundle of gear!) They had been a bit worried knowing we had been up at the pond in a bad southeaster, and as we were due out that day were walking in to make sure we were alright. We were grateful for their concern, but relieved to see that they carried their fishing rods with them. After giving us a hand by carrying the canoe down the portage, they went off to fish the big trout pool.

After such a full day it was pure joy to drift down the last peaceful bends in the warm evening sun. And so ended the fulfillment of a dream, the satisfaction of a great curiosity and the overcoming of a challenge. Western Brook Pond, the fish-shaped bit of blue on the map of Newfoundland, had come to life. Every twist and contour hung with memories to last a lifetime.

The Gorge in Winter

It takes a long, steady, very cold spell to set firm ice on a pond as deep as Western Brook Pond, so only occasionally is there a chance to see the gorge in all its winter splendour. One such winter, three of us walked in on snowshoes, over the plain and over the big open section of the pond. By way of precaution, we had a long rope with us and, spreading it to its full length, walked at the ends and the middle of it so as to spread our weight and have a lifeline in case of a break in the ice. Park researchers have found that the water of Western Brook Pond doesn't reach its maximum temperature for the year until November so, this being March, we figured it might still retain some of its "warmth" and hence our precautions. But although the ice was patchy and we had to scramble over a large pressure ridge in the middle, we did not have any trouble crossing the four miles of ice to the gorge.

As we reached Western Brook Hill, which stands at the entrance to the gorge on the south side, we came upon the big pug marks of a lynx and could see where he had come right down a gully from a lair high up on the hill. There was a thin cover of snow on the ice so we could see where he had followed the shore into the gorge. The prints were so fresh we thought we might catch sight of him, but he was more likely watching us from some safe spot.

Inside the shelter of the hill we stopped for a boil-up. Tea never tasted so good, well boiled in an old juice can over a few sticks!

The ice inside the gorge was much better than out on the open pond, so we walked on till we rounded the first big bend and could see all along the main cliffs on the south side. The sun was brilliant and only a faint haze of snow crystals in the air reduced the knife-edged sharpness of the cliff tops. The patterns in the cliffs were highlighted by the snow, so that the crags and fissures, the vast unbroken slabs, the leaning pinnacles, and the vertical dykes that seamed the cliffs from top to bottom, all showed up in sharp relief.

We would have liked to go further, and could have done so with cross-country skis, but with our slower snowshoes we had gone as far as we could. There are not many winters when the ice of Western Brook Pond is reliable, so we were lucky to have this thrilling experience of seeing the great freshwater fjord under snow.

Cliff Tops and Caribou Country

The trail to Western Brook Pond and the boat tours had been established for several years when some rock climbing friends of ours spent a few weeks exploring the various routes up the clefts and gullies of the gorge. Their accounts of the cliff tops were thrilling and opened up for us a whole new dimension of the great pond. To reach the tops became our next objective.

We could not match our friends' ability as climbers, but they reckoned we could manage one of their routes, which was really just a long steep scramble up a watercourse. Only the top few feet required any real rock climbing.

This watercourse is one of the most dramatic gullies on the south side, a narrow one starting from a small beach, the only beach in the length of the gorge. The cleft runs up beside an immense slab of sheer smooth granite and the top of it is close to the main cliffs.

We chose the middle of June, close to the summer solstice, at a time when the moon was going to be full. This time we avoided the troublesome journey up Western Brook and carried the canoe over the trail to the end of Long Steady, making a second trip for our packs. We launched the canoe there and paddled up the peaceful steady and the top section of the river. The weather was perfect and the huge sheet of water as calm as a mill pond.

Once in the gorge we spent a long time out on the water studying every inch we could see of the gully before making camp on the little pebble beach below it. On this, the shaded side of the gorge, patches of snow still lay among the brilliant new green of the birches. Everything shone with spring's renewal and birdsong echoed everywhere. As we cooked our supper, the low sun caught the falling mist of a tiny waterfall high above us and turned it into a brilliantly wavering spectrum of colour.

Knowing that the moon would be full in this crystal-clear sky, we dared not sleep in case we missed it. Daylight lasted until 10:30, and it was midnight before it was dark enough for the moonlight to take over. Dead tired, we struggled out and launched the canoe. Under the south cliffs we were in deep shadow; opposite, the north cliffs were as clear as day. We paddled out into the moonlight, so awed by the stillness and the silence that we hardly dared speak above a whisper. High above us two or three gulls, ghostly in the moonlight, flew quietly in to their nests on the cliffs. Slowly and silently, hardly disturbing the black stillness of the water, we paddled eastward for a mile or more, drinking in this incredible scene. Eventually we returned to the beach and our sleeping bags for what was left of the night.

Because of our midnight outing, we were late starting in the morning. Realizing that we could not make it right to the top and back in a day, we nonetheless decided to climb as far as time would allow.

Fed by melting snow, the little stream was a rushing cascade that leapt and tumbled over a mass of rocks and boulders and we rock-hopped and scrambled, criss-crossing the stream to make our way upward. At first we were surrounded by thick trees and bush, but as we reached the narrow cleft below the granite wall there was neither soil nor space for trees and though it was very steep we could climb faster. Seen here at close quarters, the vast uninterrupted rock face was awe inspiring. As we climbed higher, the gully became a chaos of boulders and the stream made wild leaps among them. Here we decided to turn back but we were well satisfied to have reached a point three quarters of the way to the top. Taking a long rest before the climb down — which would be more hazardous than the ascent — we gazed out of the cleft at the sunlit cliffs on the north side and the dark water of the pond far below.

The whole expedition, with the midsummer night's moonlit paddle on the still pond and this magnificent climb, was a unique experience, perhaps the most memorable of the many we have had in Gros Morne. But the cliff tops were still to be conquered!

Tantalizingly, Park people would talk casually of being taken up there by helicopter for their various purposes. We couldn't help envying them, but we still wanted to get there on foot!

Always having an ear cocked for news of approaches that could be taken, we heard that a group of Explorer Scouts had hiked the whole round of the tops surrounding Western Brook Pond, taking five or six days of hard bush-whacking to do it. As their navigator was from Woody Point we were able to hear the details of their exploit firsthand. Maps we had already, and marked in their route to the south cliffs. But air photographs were essential to be able to find the right way in to the mountains among the many old woods trails crossing the coastal plain, and these we obtained from Ottawa.

Before setting out we got all the information we could about the route from local men, but after the first sections that they could point to, the wanderings of the trail were impossible to describe. In fact, we only discovered the important section of the trail that avoids a broad belt of tuck when we were on our way out after a later, second trip to the cliffs! No one could describe its tortuous route, or how to find its beginning.

Much of the climb was through steep but open woods, but near the top these became a dense belt of tuckamore which we had to struggle through. But once clear of this, much of the plateau is relatively easy walking and we could see for miles. However, every dip and gully between the ridges is filled with tuck, sometimes spruce, two or three feet deep, but often fir, which grows head high and more, and is like a goblin forest, snatching, pricking, tripping and trapping you at every step. Temper wears thin, clothes get torn, and progress is painfully slow.

This part of the Long Range is home to great numbers of caribou. Every exposed ridge and level is rich in caribou moss, and as the animals are constantly on the move from one grazing patch to another they make trails of a sort. On open ground these are clear to see and well marked with droppings, but one has to develop an eye for the places where the caribou trails enter the bands of tuck. After a few yards their track becomes invisible, but as you move along, it is your feet rather than your eyes that pilot you through and out the other side.

To get to the cliffs and have time to enjoy them, one needs to camp at least two nights along the way, but with weather so uncertain on the Long Range one should have at least four day's food in case of having to hole up and wait for the clouds to lift. Near those cliff tops, which are as sharp and sudden as the side of a box, one cannot risk moving about in minimal visibility.

We had one such morning after a night of thick mist. The place where we camped was evidently a nesting area for willow ptarmigan and all night long they called to each other in the most neighbourly fashion, as though checking that everyone was alright and not lost in the mist. When dawn came we were blanketed in solid fog and feared that our precious days might all be spent waiting for it to lift. But by mid-morning the sun began to burn it off and we were able to set out. As we approached the gorge, the mist boiled up over the lip and as we got closer we looked down into a vast swirling, seething cauldron.

It cleared to a brilliant day and we explored all along the main section of the cliffs, stopping to loaf and gaze and try to take it all in, for there was both great and small to see. All of us had been impressed before by great cliffs in other places, from the sheer cliffs of Bell Island in Conception Bay to Helgoland, to the Shetland Isle of Foula, but nothing had prepared us for this breathtaking spectacle. Not only the extraordinary sharpness of the edges, but the proximity of the corresponding cliffs across the water had a drama and a beauty all their own. A nearby summit is over 2400 feet; the cliff tops are not much lower. With the surface of the pond no more than a hundred feet above sea level, the cliffs themselves fall nearly 2200 feet! In places, a solid overhang allowed one to look straight down a cliff face — no place for anyone prone to vertigo!

When the tour boat went by below, no more than a dot on the water, we wondered if the people aboard could see us. If they could, they may have wondered if the moving specks against the sky were caribou, and our waving arms antlers!

View from the cliff top: the expanse of Western Brook Pond, the distant coastal plain and the Gulf of St. Lawrence.

Alpine wildflowers grew in profusion, some in unexpected places. Creamy diapensias were thick along the very lip of the sharp granite edges and tossed and blew continually in the breeze. All the berry flowers were out, including the rose-like white flowers of the bakeapples (cloudberries). Heaths and heathers of several kinds and the lovely mountain avens flourished in this high and windy habitat.

Over the rolling plateau and up toward the caribou calving area known as Big Level were patches of snow, and on many of them we could see small groups of caribou enjoying the cool footing and relief from the flies. On one of our two trips there were four of us and a Labrador retriever. Walking across a level barren, we attracted the attention of a young female caribou and stood still to see what she would do. The dog, who went back and forth keeping his people together, drew her toward us like a magnet. Taking a wide sweep, the caribou closed in gradually to about fifty yards, then suddenly caught our scent and was gone like the wind. That evening, our tents aroused the curiosity of a big stag, and we watched from a distance as he carefully investigated them. People here say caribou "can't believe their eyes," and indeed their poor eyesight and curiosity must have made them easy game.

103

Tempted by the fine weather, we set off to extend our expedition to include a look at Baker's Brook Pond before returning. But within a very short time the wind had changed, and with it the weather. Raindrops began to spatter and as the temperature dropped sharply they turned to driving sleet which stung and battered us. Before we could find a reasonable place to pitch a tent we were soaked, and since it was still possible to make the downhill return trip all in one, we decided to do so.

Our car stood by the house of some friends and, arriving there after dark, we were glad to see the house was still bright with lights. They welcomed us with all the hospitality of the west coast, and soon, warm and dry, we were sitting down to a great spread of tea and all that goes with a Newfoundland late night lunch. We told them of our successful trip, and they in turn recounted tales of travelling and hunting in the mountains in years gone by. It added a special quality to our experience to be able to share with them the feelings they had for their home range, every rock and gully of which they knew like their own back yard.

The High Route to Gros Morne

To hike over the Long Range plateau is to get the true feel of Gros Morne National Park. For all the variety of land and water that the Park encompasses, this high wilderness is the very heart of it. In order to keep it as a natural wilderness area, the Park has built no trails over the Long Range, and may never do so. Thus, for the true wilderness hiker the route from the head of Western Brook Pond to Gros Morne is a challenge and a rewarding hike.

The trip takes from three to five days, depending upon how fast you travel and how much you want to see along the way. But since the route takes you through thirty miles of very rough country, and weather is forever uncertain, it is advisable to be equipped for an extra few days. Topographical maps are essential for hiking over the mountains as the terrain and the innumerable small ponds are very confusing, and you need to map read with care the whole way.

One August I joined a party of naturalists led by two able guides who had made the trip earlier in the year. This was in one of the early years of the Park and no markers of any kind showed the way. The boat operator took us to the landing at the extreme end of the pond. As we passed the cliffs, all the brooks were roaring from recent heavy rain and spilled dramatically over the cliffs. To our surprise, a skein of Canada geese, about a dozen of them, were flying parallel to us below the cliff tops, apparently sheltered there from the wind. We were to see them again when we reached the top.

After disembarking we found ourselves in thick dark woods. Although we could not see out in any direction, the bottom of this gully was a dramatic place. The river which must course down it was nowhere visible, but ran deep below a tumbled bed of rocks. Several times our way was blocked by vast boulders that must at some time have rumbled down from the cliffs above. At one point the trees thinned out and we came upon an open area filled with a tall dense growth of joe pye weed through which we waded, chest deep. A tiny pond lay in its midst.

The long floor of the valley became steep and extremely rugged toward the upper end. The bottom was an impassable tangle, so we struggled and wrenched and slipped our way along, halfway up the south side, clinging to stunted trees and balancing our heavy packs as we went. We could now see the enticing cataract at the head of the valley where the river streamed over glistening red granite before disappearing underground. With a last intense effort we climbed onto a lovely little saddle above this cataract, an idyllic spot to camp, and there we thankfully downed our packs and rubbed our aching shoulders. Below us, the great pond snaked away toward the Gulf, peaceful in the failing light of evening.

Next morning, knowing the worst part of the trip was over, we set off with a will and were soon out in the open, making good speed. Our route followed a slight dip in the land and passed frequent ponds both large and small. Some of the streams ran westward to the coast, but many of them flowed east to feed tributaries of the Upper Humber River and so would eventually flow through the Humber Gorge and meet the salt water at Bay of Islands.

Camping that night we had the pleasant prospect of an easy walk without our packs next day for we planned a side trip westward to look for caribou on Big Level. We didn't see many, but followed their well-worn paths and got the feel of their high and barren habitat. The caribou we did see demonstrated their curiosity and poor eyesight by gazing stupidly at us until our scent reached them and sent them flying off in alarm.

We were strung out, following a caribou trail, when an arctic hare suddenly crossed our little column. Very casual and unafraid, he stopped by some rocks and tussocks nearby and sat down to look at us. The photographers in the group crept forward, getting amazingly close before this splendid animal decided they were close enough and casually lolloped off with a fine show of his dark grey back, pitch black ears and snow white scut. He was the largest and handsomest rabbit any of us had seen. Up here, we again met the skein of geese, now feeding among the low groundcover and making a companionable chatter among themselves.

That night the heavens opened and our nice little campsite became a swamp. Some very soggy packs had to be shouldered next morning. The next camp was to be our last. It was not far from the top end of the Ten Mile Pond valley that curves away below Gros Morne on the north side. After supper that evening, enticed by the look of this valley on the map, several of us thrust our way through the tuck to get a view down into it. It was spectacular indeed, and we saw too the terraced north face of Gros Morne. We stayed too long enjoying the scene, lost our way in the dusk and the tuck, and spent a lot of time, temper and energy finding our way back to the camp! That night we had a sharp touch of fall and in the morning all was white with hoar-frost.

Our lunch stop next day was at one of the loveliest spots I have found in the whole of the Park. From a fair-sized pond, a brook ran out, just a hundred feet or so, before rushing over a cataract and steeply down to the valley below. A dark red cliff face hung beside the brook and a mass of wildflowers covered the ground. It overlooked the whole Ten Mile Pond valley, into which other brooks fell in wild leaps. Beyond the pond lay the coastal plain, and beyond again the wide blue expanse of the Gulf of St. Lawrence. I could hardly tear myself away to follow the others down the last leg of the journey.

It was no great distance to the lip of the pass from which the Ferry Gulch would take us down to the Gros Morne trail. Below us lay the little pond where now there is a bivouac campsite, and directly across the narrow pass was the steep flank of Gros Morne. No trail had yet been built down the Ferry Gulch and it was a long hard descent to the foot of the bare mountain where we found the new and well-groomed trail that took us down to the road.

The sore feet and aching shoulders of the journey were soon forgotten, but all the things we saw and experienced — the animals and birds, the pouring rain and the white frost, and the tuckamore, surely most of all the tuckamore — keep this thirty miles of wild landscape vividly alive in my memory.

105

CHAPTER 10

The Northwest Corner

St. Paul's Inlet

The name St. Paul's seems to date from before the first English settlers, even before the French who held fishing rights on this coast from 1783 to 1904. It is shown as St. Paul's Inlet on maps from the seventeenth and eighteenth centuries, well before Captain James Cook made his survey of the coast in 1768. The Basque whalers, who used to sail up this coast in the sixteenth century to go whaling on the Labrador, may well have been the ones to name the inlet St. Paul's.

Approaching St. Paul's up the coast road from the south, one sees the community from about a mile away, its colourful houses clustered over a low rise and built low to the ground as though hunched against the wind. As in so many Newfoundland communities, the homes look small and simple, but inside nearly all have modern furnishings and equipment and are snug and comfortable. A narrow road winds between the houses, while the highway swings smoothly round the edge of the town and over the bridge.

St. Paul's is one of the few largely Roman Catholic communities in the Park area and the Catholic high school stands prominently beside the highway. Most of the Park's communities are largely Anglican and United Church (formerly Methodist); in some, the Salvation Army is strong. But recent years have seen the growth of fundamentalist churches in Newfoundland, and there is now a Pentecostal, Seventh Day Adventist, or Jehovah's Witness congregation in many communities.

In the old days, St. Paul's was a winter settlement, with nearly all the fishing families migrating in summer to their cabins at Old House Rocks, just south of the mouth of the estuary, to be near the fishing sheds and the precious plots where they grew their potatoes and vegetables. The long row of sheds, wharves, ramps and cabins lies parallel to the highway, on the shore just below the cliffs. It is a very busy place in summer, especially during the lobstering season. Today, although many families still enjoy being there and use their cabins and gardens, they live year-round in St. Paul's itself.

Old House Rocks is exposed to the open Gulf. To provide some protection for their boats, each two or three fishermen have created their own tiny harbour by rolling large boulders out into a protective arc. Within this scant protection they moor their dories.

St. Paul's has no natural harbour for larger boats and only small fishing boats can navigate the channels of the estuary and pass through the narrows to find shelter in the inlet. It is therefore surprising to find that, for many years in the nineteenth century, two Halifax firms had agents and premises there, buying salt cod and herring. In the more recent past, lobsters were canned in great quantities. All these products must have been ferried out through the shallow estuary to vessels anchored outside. Now the fish is sold directly to the plant at Cow Head and lobsters are collected in trucks.

Situated on this harsh shore, with settlements far apart, the St. Paul's people gained a reputation as great walkers. They thought nothing of trudging the six boggy miles to Cow Head, or walking twice that distance down the shore to visit friends in Sally's Cove. In those days, crossing the narrows where the bridge now stands, the outflow of the main inlet could be deep and fast. The first Anglican clergyman, the Reverend Rule, travelling his immense parish on foot in the 1860s, vividly described having to ballast himself with a large rock held over his head so as not to be swept away by the current as he set off for Cow Head!

For today's visitors, both the estuary and the inlet have much to offer. The estuary is probably the best area in the Park to see shore birds and ducks. It also has a wealth of saltmarsh plants, including samphire which reddens whole areas with its strange growth. Above the narrows the inlet widens into a brackish lake some nine miles long. It is a fine trip in a boat or canoe as the inlet meets the foot of the mountains and the scenery is magnificent.

The beautiful inlet of St. Paul's.

It was a day of silvery light and dead calm water when we paddled in in the canoe. Close to the south shore we watched the black reflections of the hills slowly wavering as we passed. At the head of the inlet we found a group of harbour seals loafing around, obviously enjoying themselves by the river mouth. They gazed at us with big watery eyes and, since our canoe made no sound or disturbance, they showed little fear. Once very common in Newfoundland's bays and inlets, the harbour seal population is now much reduced as fishermen, who regard them as a menace to the fishery, have killed them in great numbers.

The river that runs in at the head of the inlet is about a mile long and drains two beautiful ponds set deep in a glacier-scoured valley. We had hoped to make our way in there, either on foot through the woods or up the river with the canoe, but the sky blackened suddenly and we had no choice but to head back to St. Paul's.

As we paddled out, the rain began and soon became the heaviest downpour we had ever been out in. The water of the inlet was beaten flat by the barrage of huge drops which bounced as though they were hitting concrete, and we had to keep bailing the canoe as we paddled. Soaked through, we made the best speed we could. The bridge we aimed for looked very distant, and periodically disappeared altogether, blotted out by the rain.

About half way there, a trap-skiff suddenly loomed out of the mist, heading for us. At the tiller was a kindly fisherman who had seen us leave and took pity on our long wet paddle back down the pond. The canoe was hauled aboard and we travelled with it resting across the gunwhales of the boat. Fishermen thoroughly mistrust these fragile craft and I am sure he felt we were unsafe, as well as wet! We were thankful for the ride and saw in his kindness yet one more example of the concern for people out in the elements that is the undying legacy of the long tough history of human survival on the coast.

It was years later that I had the luck to see that beautiful inner valley from a helicopter. But the experience was so fleeting and unreal that I still hope to see those dramatic hillsides and high white waterfall from my accustomed viewpoint — a canoe on the water!

Cow Head and Shallow Bay

The most northerly of the enclave communities within the Park, Cow Head is one with a lot of character. Opinions vary about the origin of the name Cow Head. Some say the shape of the peninsula, or its shape on the map, suggests one. But early records have been found that refer to a large colony of walrus on the headland and, as these animals were often known as sea cows at that time, this seems the most likely origin of the name.

Captain James Cook made extensive notes about the potentials of Cow Head as a fishing harbour when he surveyed the coast in 1768 and, although the English did not settle there for another seventy years, the success of the fishery has borne out his opinion. In recent years both the lobstering and the off-shore fishery have been good and the Cow Head fish plant is a busy one.

The Head, which is nearly an island but has a narrow, low isthmus joining it to the mainland, has always been the main settlement. People who lived out there and fished all summer would have small, snug houses on Winterside for the winter months. But since the coming of roads and vehicles, all the permanent homes are now on the mainland and the Head has only the fish plant, the harbour, and a few cottages.

The promontory is quite high and varied. Criss-crossed with paths and trails, it is fun to explore and offers rewarding short hikes for families. There are usually lots of sheep and a few ponies grazing, and on the seaward cliffs is the smallest lighthouse I have ever seen.

There are traces of ancient human habitation on the headland and it is one of the places on the coast where people are known to have lived off the sea and the land since ancient times.

As with most settlements along this coast, the most common names in the telephone book are those of the very early English settlers who came in the first half of the nineteenth century. Payne and Hutchings have always been the main family names in Cow Head. A small museum in the town contains some interesting artifacts and much local history researched by people of the area. It is well worth a visit.

North of the Cow Head peninsula are two sweeping arcs of beach divided by Belldowns Point. The northern one, Shallow Bay, a beautiful stretch of sandy beach some three miles long, lies just within the limits of the Park. It's northern tip, known as Lower Head, is formed of the same hard, jagged breccia that forms the shoreline along many parts of this coast. Behind the high dunes the forest struggles for survival as the prevailing westerlies engulf the trees in sand. The dead ones stand for years as silver skeletons among the dunes.

A fine surf, not too deep, makes Shallow Bay one of the best places for a dip in the sea. In fact, when the tide comes in over sun-warmed sand it is amazing how warm the water can be! It is a lovely place to spend a day swimming, hiking barefoot, building sandcastles, or just plain loafing. The picnic site and changing rooms are at Belldowns Point, and there is a nice campground at the back of the dunes. Snowshoe hares have become particularly tame there and nibble grass between the tents as though they were cotton-tail bunnies!

Just off Belldowns Point lie the White Rock Islets, and off Cow Head another smaller island called Stearin Island. These low sandy islands are nesting areas for common terns, known in Newfoundland as stearins. All along the shore their harsh cries can be heard as they fish the inshore waters. Their graceful lilting flight makes them seem lighter than air, until they dive like ligtning to catch some tiny fish for their young. The two nesting colonies are now carefully protected.

Belldowns Point

Until recent years when it was phased out and the people were relocated to make way for Park facilities, Belldowns Point was another attractive little community, very independent and neat. One house I knew there was a perfect example of an old-fashioned home such as hardly exists anymore. It was a delight to visit. Every surface shone with glistening paint. An old fashioned wood-burning kitchen range gleamed like silver, as did every pot and pan. On the polished floor were some of the best and most finely hooked rugs I have ever seen, each one different and each designed by the maker, the woman of the house.

Another of this lady's skills was the knitting of the distinctive west coast design of fisherman's sweater known locally as a guernsey. Before the circular needles of today became available, these sweaters were knitted in the round on many short sock needles and the only place where a sewing needle was used in the whole sweater was where the shoulders were grafted. A few years ago, she would have spun her own wool as well. The knitting was fine and firm, almost like tweed, so that neither fishing gear in the boat nor twigs in the woods would catch in it, nor wind and spray go through it easily. A guernsey would last through many years of hard work.

I always think of this nice old home when I go to Belldowns Point. It stood where the parking lot is now and was sheltered by a little belt of trees. All around it the bright green grass was nibbled short by the sheep. The fences, sheds, tidy woodpile and signs of work going on all bespoke a well-ordered and self-sufficient family. It is sad that no way could have been found to preserve this old home which was such an outstanding example of the older way of life.

CHAPTER 11

North of the Boundary Line

Parsons Pond

As the coast sweeps northward the Long Range Mountains lie farther and farther inland until, at the Park's boundary, they are some ten miles across the coastal plain. On any clear day, however, they are a remarkable sight with their extraordinary jumble of steep and contorted valleys. One of their most rugged and dramatic sections is at the head of Parsons Pond.

This beautiful tidal inlet was at one time planned for inclusion in the Park, but because of a small oil deposit that may some day become commercially viable, the boundary was set a few miles to the south. It is a marvelous ten mile trip by boat to the foot of the mountains.

One early summer day we sailed in with our eleven foot lug-sail dinghy and camping gear. Launching *Bip* by the fishing wharves, we picked up some useful information about the pond from the lads who watched us getting ready. Under sail we would need an incoming tide to be able to pass upstream under the bridge; then we would have to stay clear of the shallow areas in the estuary, and of the submerged rocks along the south side of the pond. We were lucky, for a strong southwest wind came up and we sailed under the bridge in fine style and fairly tore up the main part of the pond.

The mountain range got more impressive as we got closer. At the head of the pond we could see two hillocks, both of which would be good viewpoints if we could reach their tops through the thick scrub. One stands by the main river that flows in at the head of the pond, the location of a few fishing cabins; the other is a little to the south, and at its foot we found an idyllic place to camp, a little meadow beside a meandering stream. All around the alder beds rang with birdsong.

Our camp was all set up by late afternoon so we set out to attempt to climb the little hill nearby. Unfortunately it was protected by a mass of tangled undergrowth, so instead we rowed *Bip* up the stream as far as we could go, pulled the boat ashore, and walked on through tall open woods. A stand of big dead birches, riddled with woodpecker holes, was occupied by a horde of tree swallows, flashing about like blue streaks. Deep in the moist woods we came upon trilliums, the first we had ever seen in Newfoundland. Modest, small and greeny-white, they must have been nodding trilliums.

Gazing up at the mountains, now less than a mile away, we noticed a ridge above us that was actively crumbling along its sharp and jagged edge; below it huge scree slopes of pinkish rock looked unweathered and newly fallen. Later that night we were woken up, spooked and scared, by crashing noises, only to realize they were made by rocks crashing down the hillside. Visible on the skyline, this ragged ridge can be seen from the road.

Next morning was misty and threatening rain. We rowed across to the main river at the base of the other little hill where some anglers showed us where to find the path that led to the top. The path followed the upper edge of a scree slope and there we found lovely wildflowers just coming into bloom: tiny mauve primulas, two or three inches high; patches of mountain avens; and yellow moccasin orchids at the stage where their yellow pouches were swollen and shiny but their twisty, brown, whisker-like petals had not yet opened. At the foot of a cliff we passed a large, deep cave that has been known as Bear Cave since the time a bear took up residence there.

From the top we looked down onto the twists of the rushing river. Barely a mile long, it ran out of an inner pond set deeply in the mountains, much of it hidden from our view by the ragged ridge. Seen in the mist, that inner pond was a magical and tantalizing sight. In all directions ran steep valleys , and the map showed the sides of the hidden section to be almost vertical. When the mist turned to rain, we took shelter in the Bear Cave and, gazing out, wondered if we would ever be able to bring the canoe in here and somehow get it onto that wonderful inner pond.

After a wet and windy night, the morning was calm and sunny — too calm for dinghy sailors! With only an occasional puff of wind, we rowed most of the way down the pond, but in our gentle progress saw many birds on the water. A loon with her young ones made great efforts to distract our attention from them by acting as though she was injured.

Contoured valleys and precipitous slopes surround the wonderful inner pond above Parsons Pond.

We followed her as she floundered and squawked in the water. Eventually, when we were safely out of the way of her chicks, she flew off. A raft of golden-eyes, their handsome black and white plumage glinting in the sun, was not disturbed by our passing, but shy black ducks flew up like arrows to avoid us. Close to the community the muddy banks of the estuary were the nesting place of hundreds of bank swallows that swooped and circled over the water, catching insects in the calm evening air.

Whenever we were in that area afterwards, walking on the cliffs north of Shallow Bay or driving up the highway, we would look across at those rugged mountains, still hoping that one day we could get onto that marvelous inner pond with the canoe.

Many years later some friends who have explored most of the accessible waters of the Park with their outboard motorboat, were intrigued by our account of Parsons Pond and the inner pond set deep among the mountains. Together we undertook to find out if there was any way to get a canoe in there.

Calling at the general store close to the harbour, we soon found that the storekeeper was quite familiar with the end of the pond and knew of an old trail that led over the ridge we had seen. He thought it might serve as a portage for the canoe, though he suspected it might be rather grown in and hard to find. The river, he said, was too steep to navigate.It seemed as if there was a good chance of being able to get in to the inner pond with the canoe, but even if portaging proved impossible, we could at least walk over the ridge and so reach the shore of that tantalizing pond. We soon planned a joint expedition.

With the motorboat laden with camping gear, and towing the canoe, we made our way carefully through the shallows. Once on the main pond we motored steadily toward the mountains. This time we made our camp on a sand-spit at the mouth of the stream. It was conveniently furnished with a huge birch trunk, long stranded and smoothly weathered, which served us as both bench and picnic table. In the afterglow of a sunset that lit the mountains, we sat long over our camp fire, planning the next day's expedition and feeling somewhat daunted by the sight of the steep ridge over which we would have to carry the canoe.

But when, next morning, after some searching, we found the beginning of the trail hidden among the alders we were delighted to find that it had recently been cut out and a brand new small dory lay in the woods waiting to be carried over the trail — a most encouraging sight. The trail was very steep, but with four of us taking turns carrying the canoe we made it over the top and down the far side in less than an hour. Here we found the river more tranquil so one of the party waded upstream with the canoe while the rest followed the trail.

Emerging suddenly from the woods at the shore of the pond, we saw before us a breathtaking scene: the water was as still as glass, the only disturbance a gentle V left by a merganser and her ducklings which swam off to avoid us, the only sounds the low quacks she made to keep her little family together. Once out on the water the effect of its glassy smoothness became almost supernatural for the whole sky was reflected in its surface. We had the eerie sensation of paddling through the sky and in and out among the clouds for the surface of the water itself could not be seen.

As we passed the ragged-topped mountain, we saw that its crest was a sharp ridge that fell away on both sides at an amazing angle. It was this ridge that had hidden much of the inner pond from our view. Once around the point, the narrow gash between the mountains filled the still water with its reflection. The steep inclines on either side were identically mirrored and the images that met at water level were like the beaks of two huge birds. On this calm morning the terrain and its reflections were one of the most astonishing sights we had ever seen.

We had but a brief glimpse of its mirrored perfection before a gust ruffled the surface. Lost in wonder, we paddled on slowly, gazing up at the green heights around us. To the east was a remarkable rockfall which we had seen with binoculars from the coast. Being pure white, we had taken it for an extraordinary cascade of water; but here we saw that it was a wide chute of glistening white and pink crystalline rock swept clean of vegetation from the crest of the ridge to the water's edge. A tiny stream which fell in a cascade from another angle met the lower part of the chute and rattled over the shining rocks at its foot.

Back at the river outlet we rested on the beach, soaking up the sun and the scenery while the second pair of paddlers explored the pond. The return portage seemed easy after the success of our venture. The inner pond had proved to be even more remarkable than we had expected from our first misty view years before, and for all of us the effort it took to get there was richly rewarded.

That evening we enjoyed a visit from a boatload of local people who were staying at their cabin by the main river. They told us the name of the little hill close to our camp. On its side, the scree and the green groundcover created a neat figure 17, so Seventeen is what it is called. We had noticed another curious feature of this hill as we approached in the motorboat: the various rock faces and indentations of the hillside make a large and remarkably lifelike pig's head, with ears, eyes, snout and jowls all as clear as if they had been carved. Our visitors told us of a hunting trail which winds round the back of Seventeen and into another steep-sided valley with two ponds set deep between its walls. We explored this beautiful valley next morning before we broke camp and headed for home.

It is, in a way, a pity that this wonderful section of terrain could not have been included in Gros Morne National Park, but nothing will spoil its splendour, and, for the more venturesome who do not need Park facilities, it will always be there to be explored.

The Arches

A few miles north of Parsons Pond is a very special bit of beach. A road sign indicates The Arches Beach and a short spur of road leads you there.

Right on the tidewash is a most unusual sea stack with a series of arches which the pounding sea has carved and worn to such beautiful contours that they look almost man-made. The stack is composed of the same extremely hard rock that forms the low cliffs and shelving rock of much of the shore. It also forms the glacier-resisting barriers that underlie the low ridges crossing the coastal plain, and account for many of the belts of trees between the expanses of bog. A fine example of it can be seen at the outflow of the river from Western Brook Pond. Called breccia, it is a conglomerate that seems to be a sort of natural concrete in which are set rocks and worn pebbles from an even earlier geological time. Immeasurably long ago The Arches must have been part of such a rock barrier.

The main arch is divided into two by a pillar as solid, smooth and elegant as the bow of a ship. The ceiling, some ten to twenty feet high, is a smooth sweeping curve, and the wide double arch is some fifty feet in depth from front to back. Another, lesser arch to the north and a few small holes show where the sea's work of sculpture goes relentlessly on. The top of this remarkable piece of sea sculpture is a smooth green hummock, covered with the tough vegetation of the seashore.

The Arches, a multiple sea stack near Parsons Pond.

The beach is composed of the most amazing collection of pebbles. Four to eight inches across, they come in every stripe and colour combination, representing the enormously varied kinds of rock to be found in the area; pink speckled granite, green epidote, or white quartz sandwiched in rocks of black, gold, grey or red. All are polished smooth by the sea and where the tide washes them they shine with a marvelous array of colours. These stones are the tools with which the winter storms of thousands of years have broken through the Arches. At every tide the waves race through, pounding the rock vaults ever smoother, and ever larger.

Even on a rough day in summer the noise of the sea and the rumbling beachrocks is impressive; in a heavy onshore gale it is deafening. Only when it is calm and the tide dead low can you walk right through and look back at The Arches from the seaward side.

The Arches and the beachrocks are not the only things of interest here. This is another section of coast where earlier levels of the beach have left a green strip between the shore and the tuckamore. You can walk and beachcomb for miles along this strip with the thick wind-beaten spruce on one side, the sea on the other, and all the bric-a-brac of the Gulf in between.

This natural track, smoothed a little by passing feet, has been the only path up and down the northwest coast not just for centuries, but for thousands of years. It is a place to stop and think awhile, for this track is our direct link with all those who walked before us: Indians of unimaginable antiquity; Inuit people of a time far older than our own brief era; perhaps a few shipwrecked Vikings or Basque whalers; and only within the comparatively short span of recorded history, French and, later, English fishermen. With the desolate shore stretching on for miles, the roar of the wind and waves in one's ears, one can almost see their ancient forms slowly moving away into the mist.

CHAPTER 12

Travellers of These Same Paths

There is a natural tendency for any present inhabitant of a place to feel that its history started with his or her own ancestors. But recent years have seen such staggering discoveries in archaeology that western Newfoundland and southern Labrador are now known to have been settled by a succession of people over a span of thousands of years. The record of these ancient settlers is to be found only in bones and stone artifacts, for only since the sixteenth century is there any recorded history of this area, and much of that concerns people of quite different stock from those who live here now.

The northwest coast of Newfoundland is, for the most part, too exposed and rugged for settlement. But every few miles of its length there is a sheltering point, a peninsula, a river mouth with fertile land alongside, or a deep and protected inlet. Over the millennia a slow procession of settlers has found and used the places which offered the best chance of food, shelter and survival.

Out of the mists of time came the Maritime Archaic Indians, some of the most easterly wanderers of the people whose antecedents apparently came from Asia and slipped across the Bering Strait to spread and settle in all corners of the Americas. They lived in considerable numbers on this coast and left a wealth of artifacts, particularly at their burial ground at Port au Choix. While no house or tent sites have been found there, their cemetery has more than ninety graves. More than half of those buried there were small children, and it is in the children's graves that the greatest number of artifacts have been found.

These artifacts show the high degree of skill they had in working stone of various kinds into tools and hunting weapons. Slate was ground into long sharp blades capable of piercing the tough hide of walrus or seal; chert was chipped to form razor-sharp arrowheads and knives. Antler, bone and ivory were used to make decorative charms and amulets, fine needles and even whistles. Shells were deftly cut to reveal the beauty of the spiral and were apparently used to decorate their skin clothing. The use of Red Ochre seems to have played an important part in their ceremonies.

Although there is no more direct knowledge of these very early settlers, their graves suggest that they had quite an organized society and some form of religion and mysticism as well. Just when these people came to the island of Newfoundland is not known, but

115

carbon dating shows that they were living across the Straits in southern Labrador eight to nine thousand years ago and that they were living on the west coast, at Port au Choix and around Bonne Bay, for about a thousand years. Some three thousand years ago they seem to have mysteriously disappeared.

The Beothuks, who are known to have lived in Newfoundland from about 700 AD, had many characteristics in common with the Maritime Archaic Indians and may well have been their descendents. One of Newfoundland's greatest tragedies was the extermination of these unarmed and basically peaceful people. The last known Beothuk died in 1829.

Inuit people, of a race now referred to as Dorset Eskimo, moved gradually down the Labrador coast and then spread all around the coast of Newfoundland during the years from three thousand to thirteen hundred years ago. On this coast they had settlements and camps at Port au Choix, Cow Head, Bonne Bay and Port au Port, leaving their camp areas littered with finely made hunting and fishing tools of stone, antler and ivory. They must have been remarkably efficient hunters for the bones of whale, seal, walrus, caribou and birds have all been found at the site of their settlement at Port au Choix. The Dorset Eskimo people seem to have overlapped with the Maritime Archaic Indians and may perhaps have had something to do with their departure.

The Vikings arrived just over a thousand years ago and no one knows how far they wandered or what settlements they may have had, other than L'Anse aux Meadows. It seems unlikely, however, that such avid explorers would fail to find and use such good harbours and living places as Port au Choix, Cow Head and Bonne Bay. The Viking site at the tip of the Northern Peninsula is a wonderful spot — bleak, wild and very evocative. On a stormy day, with wind whipped sea and scudding clouds, you would hardly be surprised to catch a glimpse of these hardy Norsemen going about their business. Parks Canada maintains a very fine visitors' centre full of information and models, while outside, full-sized replicas of Norse Turf houses have been constructed. The sheepskin sleeping bags and smouldering embers in the fire pits make it seem as though the occupants had just left for their day's work.

The Basques, those hardy sailors from the Bay of Biscay, discovered the great numbers of whales in the Labrador straits and by the sixteenth century had a thriving industry and a number of whaling stations there. They were familiar with the coast of Newfoundland and theirs were the first accurately-recorded visits to the area. They made maps, drew up sailing directions, and kept records of both the whaling business and those involved in it. These remarkable records were discovered in the Spanish archives in the 1970s. Research connected them with these coasts and led to the identification of the Basque whaling station at Red Bay, Labrador, now a major Parks Canada historic site.

While the Basques went about their whaling, the French came to the west coast to fish in the spring, returning home each fall. As the English had all the fishing they needed at the time in eastern and southern Newfoundland, they gave the fishing rights on the west coast to the French in 1783 under the Treaty of Utrecht. The coast became known as the French Shore, and here they remained firmly entrenched as regular summer fishing communities until England withdrew their rights in 1904. By that time the English had been settling the west coast for a full century but the Royal Navy had seen to it that such settlers did not impinge on the rights held by the French to set up fishing premises, wharves and fish-flakes wherever they wished. When the treaty rights were withdrawn most of the French left, but a few stayed, as evidenced by the many French names all up and down this coast.

But not all who bore French names were from France. Groups of fishermen came from the island of Jersey in the English Channel and, though French by name and language, they were British citizens. Anchor Point on the Straits shore was a settlement of Jersey people. Probably because of their French language, the Jersey fishermen tended to keep rather apart. Evidently a number of Jersey crews would sail down to Bonne Bay to sell their fish and stay over a few days before returning with new supplies and gear. A large shed by the wharves at Woody Point had a bunkroom which they always used, and not only that shed but the whole place was at one time generally referred to as The Jersey Room.

Parallel in time with the early immigration and settlement of the French and the English in Newfoundland came groups of Micmac Indians from Nova Scotia. The Micmacs spread up the west coast and were living in the Bonne Bay area when the French and English arrived. Relations between the groups seem to have been quite friendly, and they engaged in a little mutual trading. In general the Micmac people and their descendents are completely integrated into the population, but they have retained several predominantly Indian communities in Newfoundland, chief among which is Conne River, Bay D'Espoir, on the south coast.

Most of today's communities on the northwest coast were settled by west country English people within the last one hundred and fifty years, and just a handful of generations span the years of accelerated transition into modern times. While their history and antecedents are well documented, this tiny slice of history is but a minute when set against the time span of active settlement by the long procession of people who have travelled these same paths before.

This natural track, smoothed a little by passing feet, has been the only path up and down the coast for thousands of years.

Index

Printed in Canada